I0478933

Black Brothers

Coloring Book

Adult Coloring Books

Aryla Publishing 2019

978-1-912675-50-0

www.arylapublishing.com

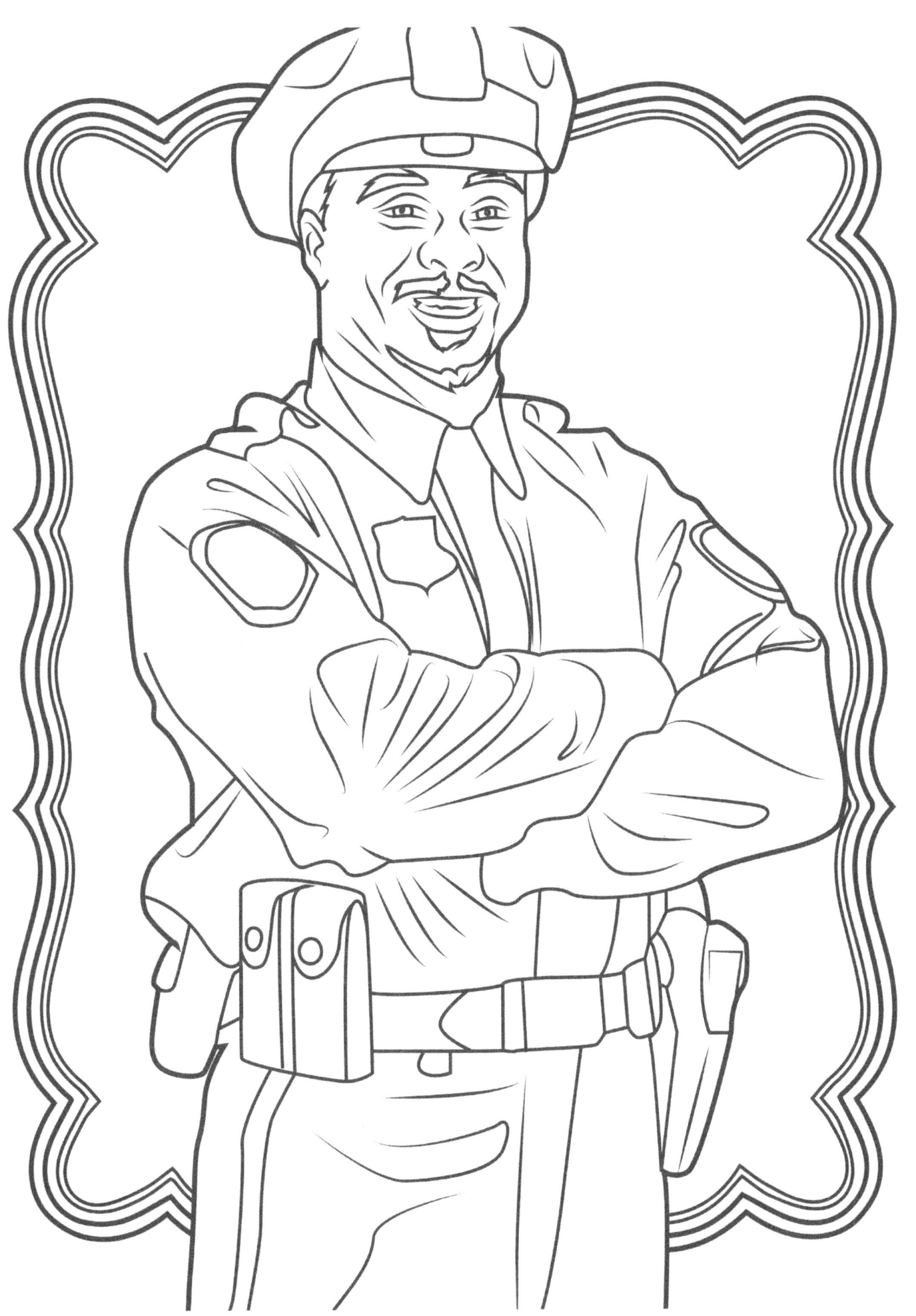

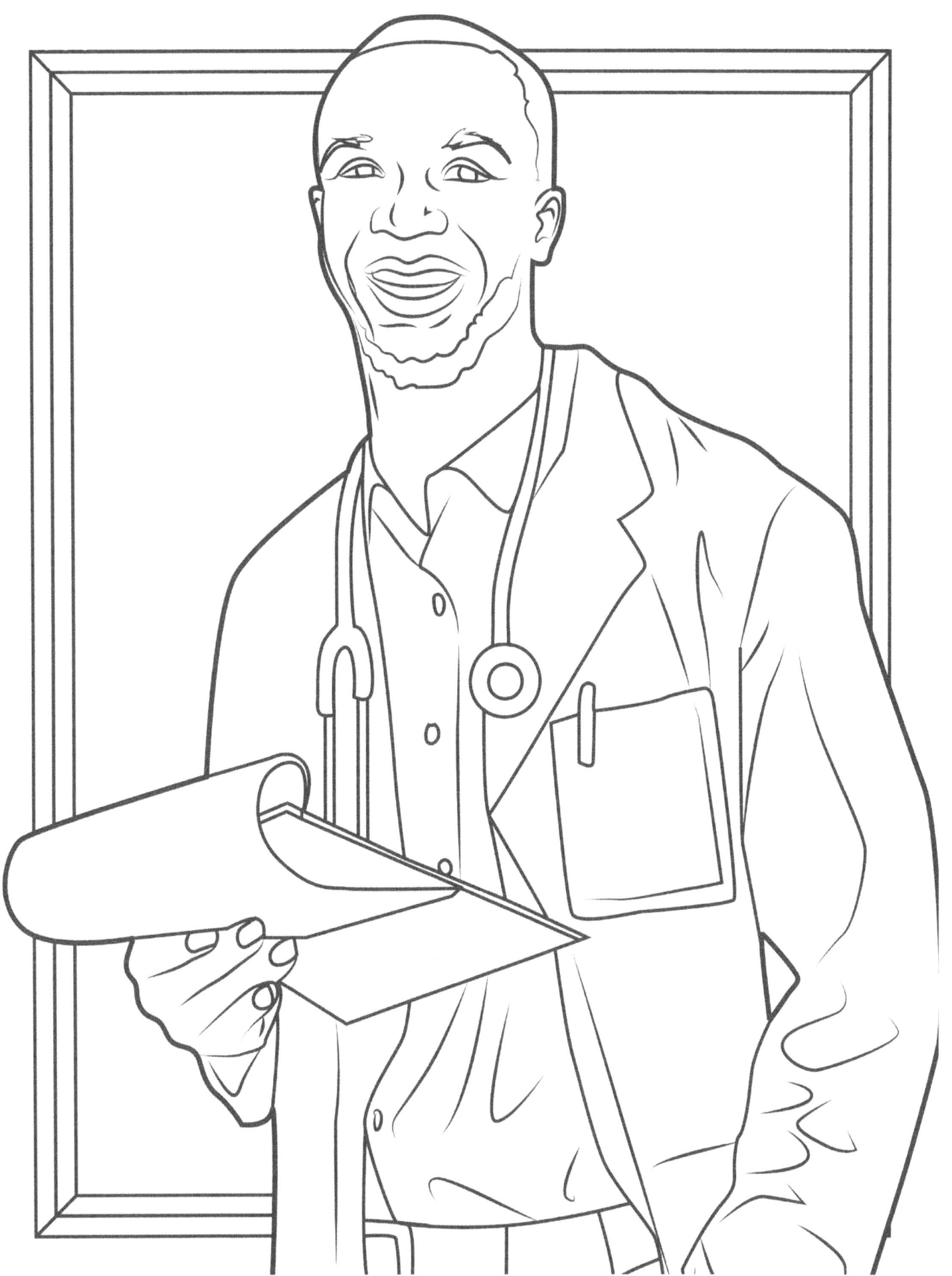

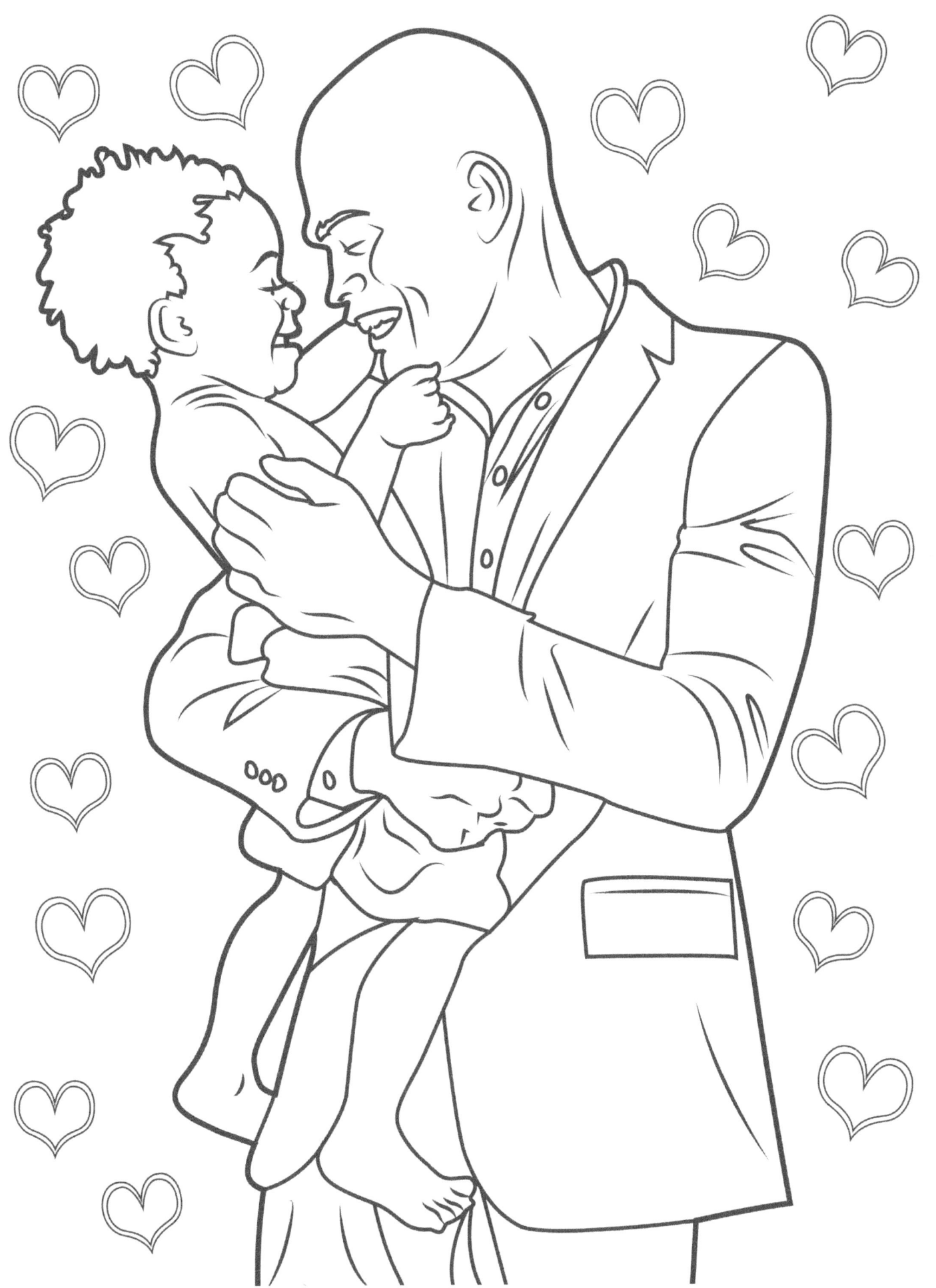

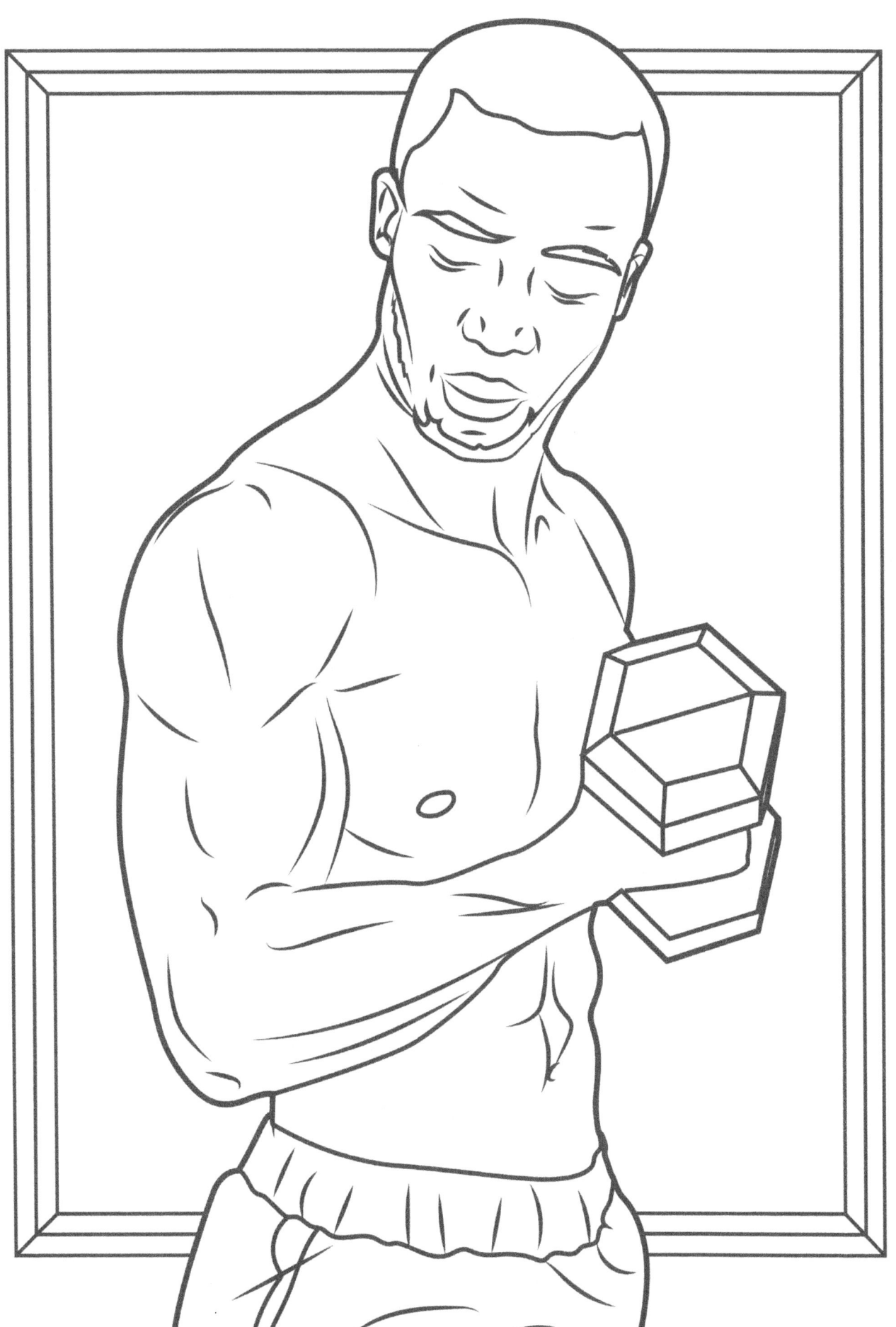

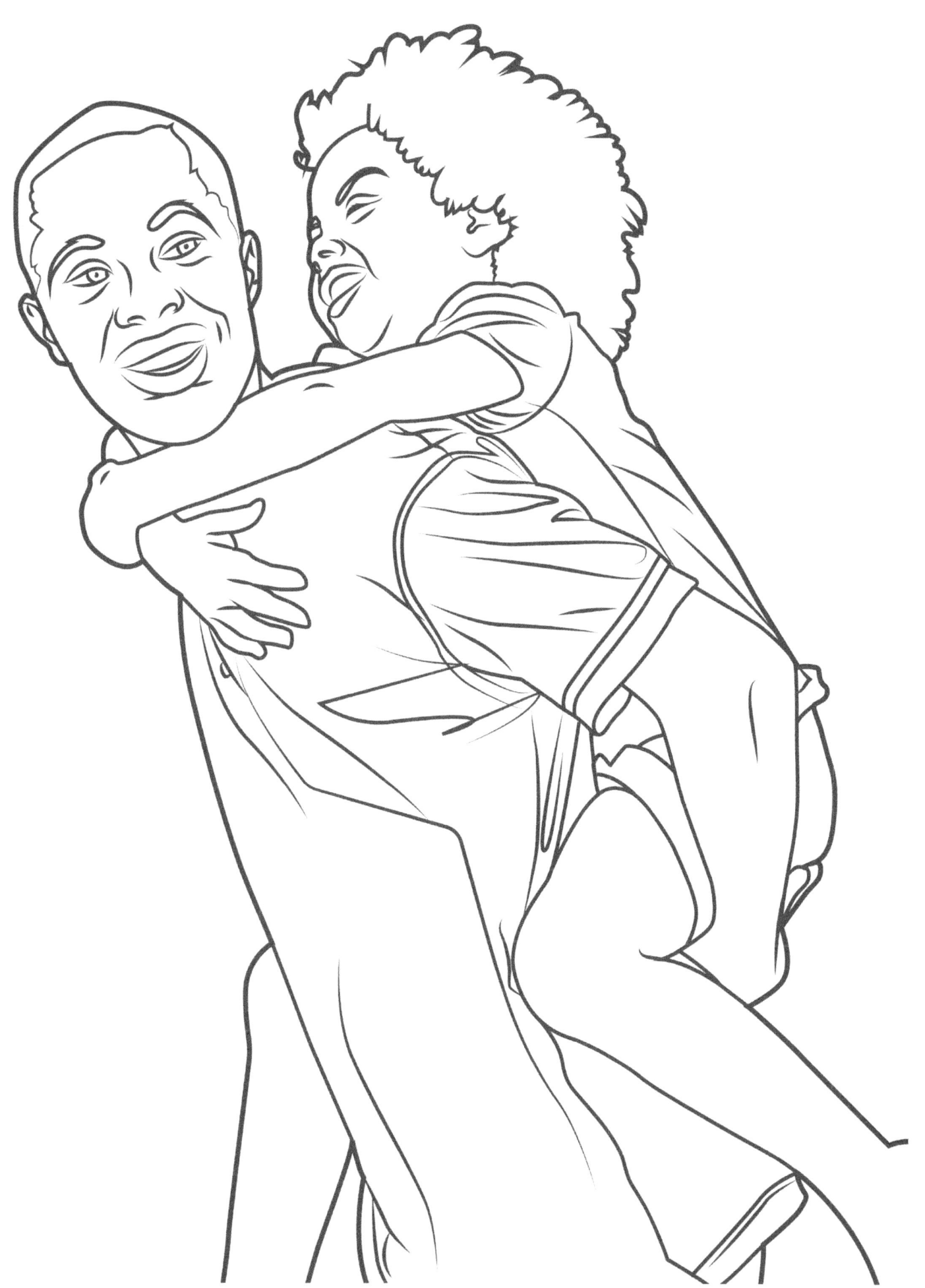

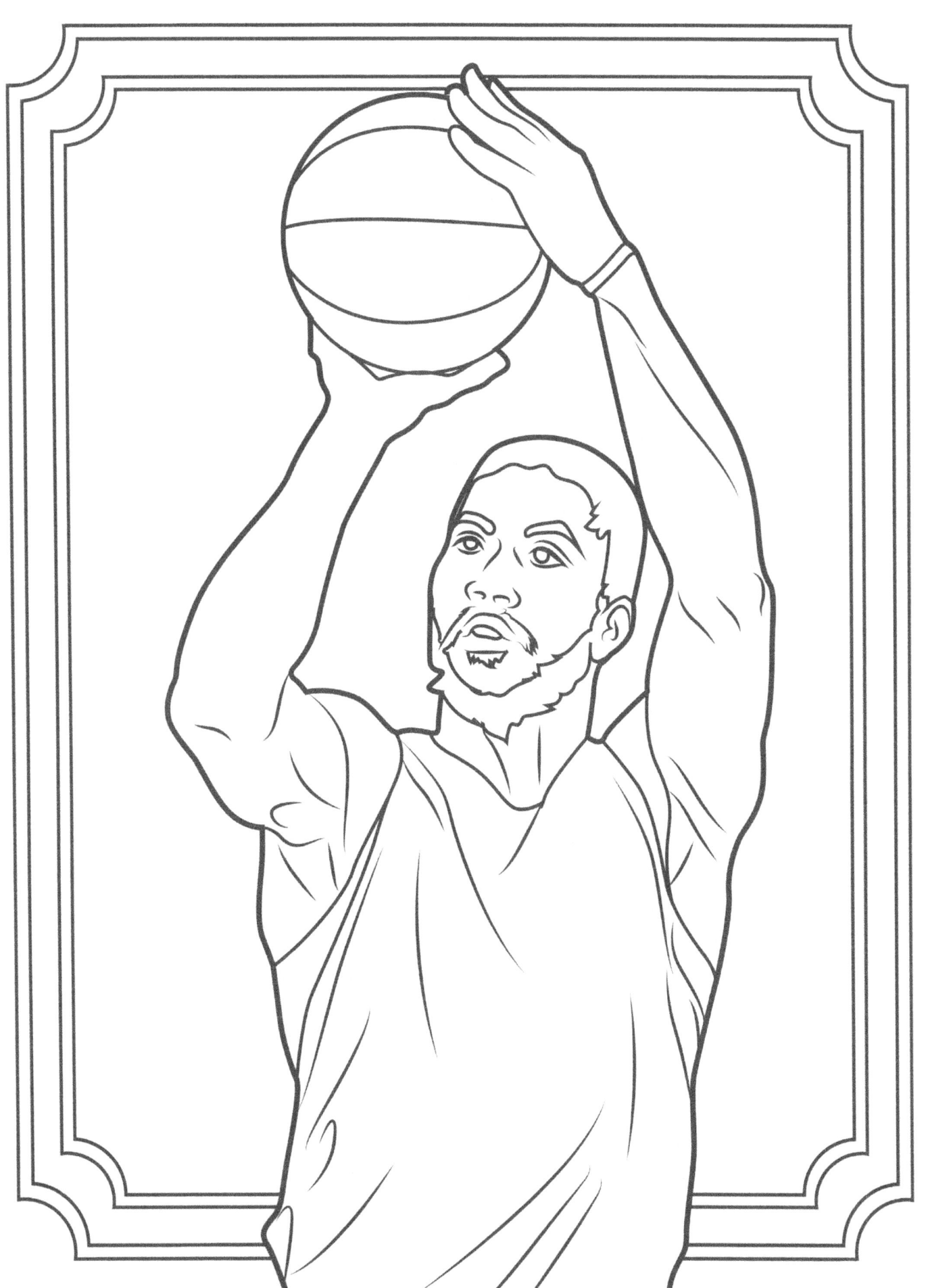

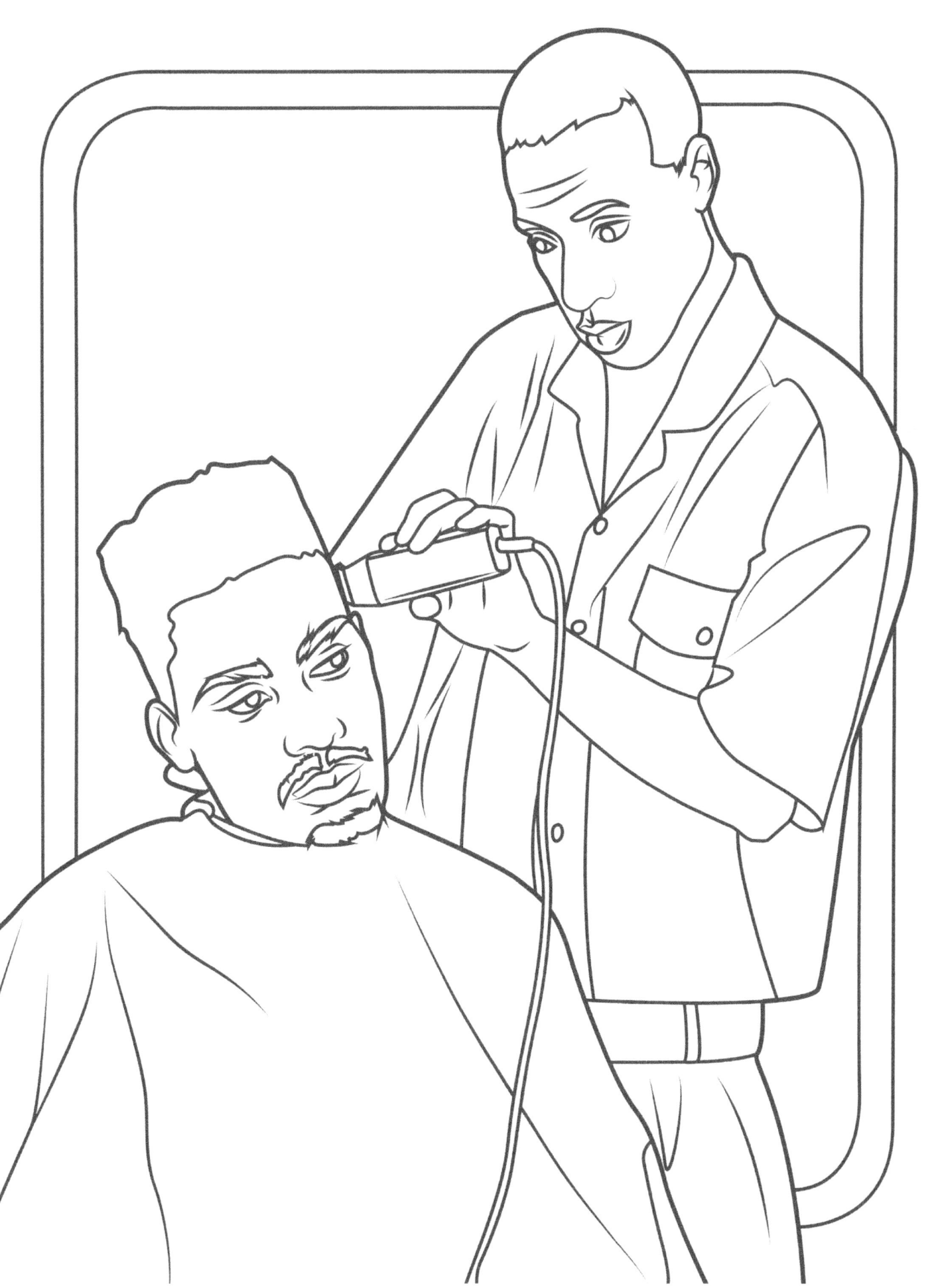

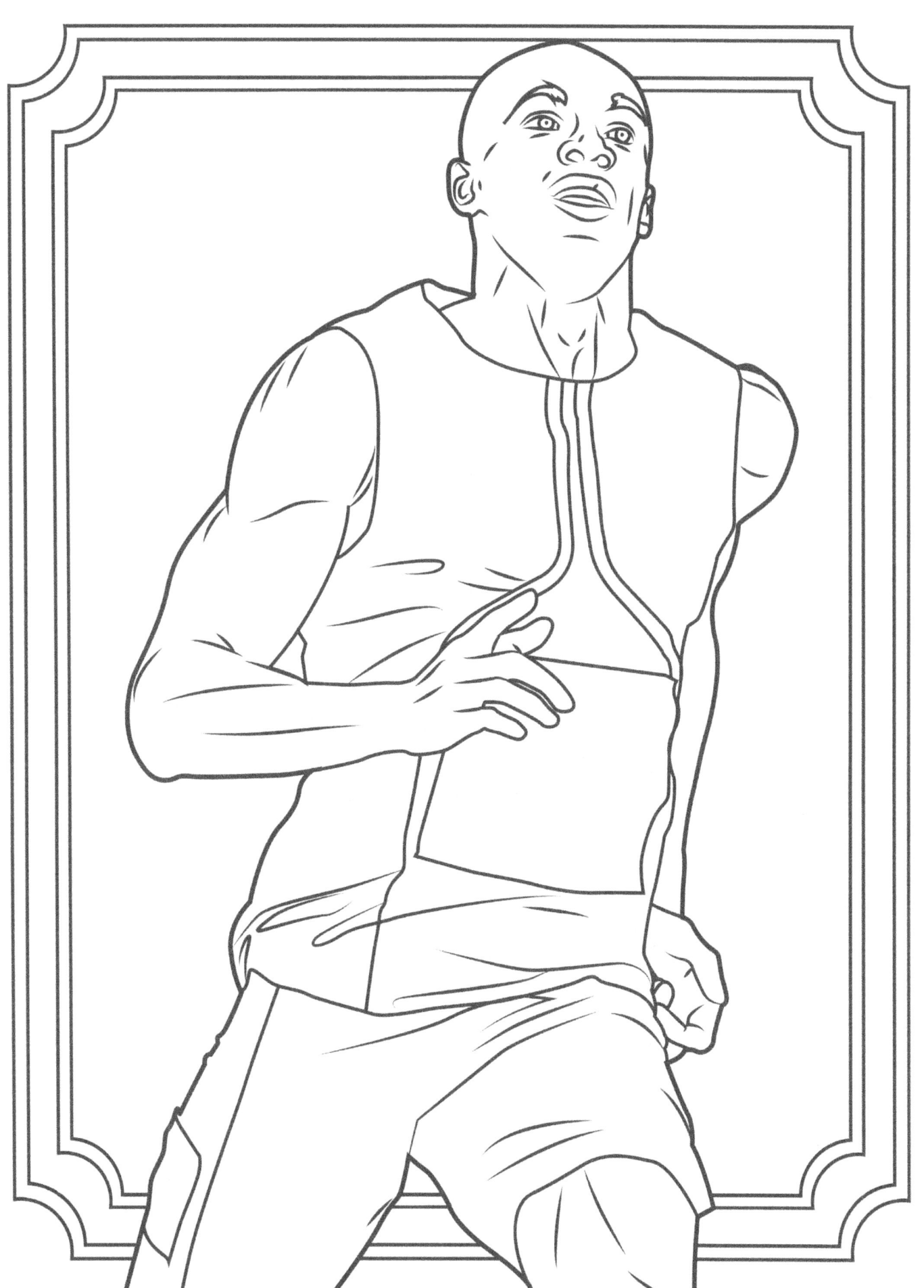

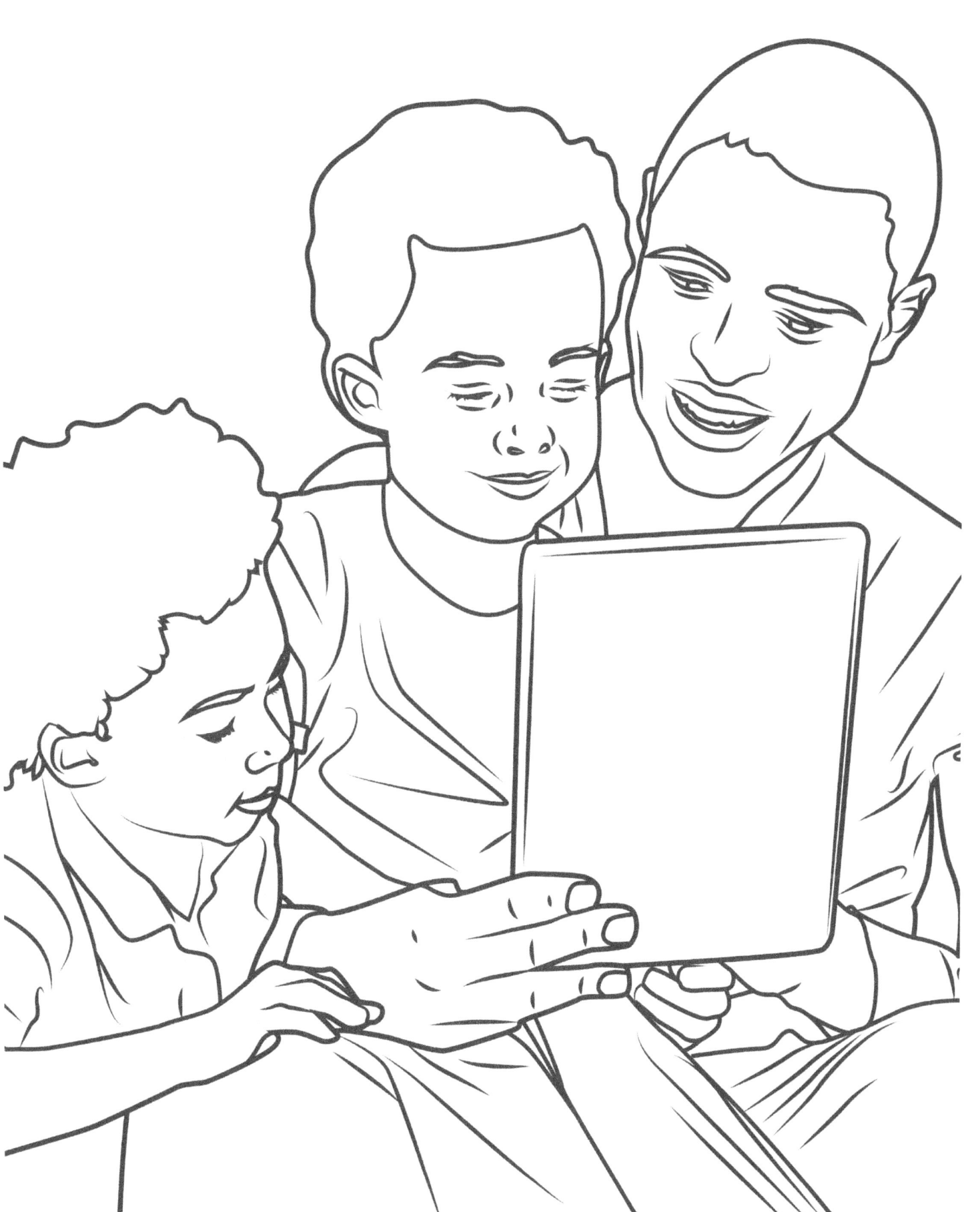

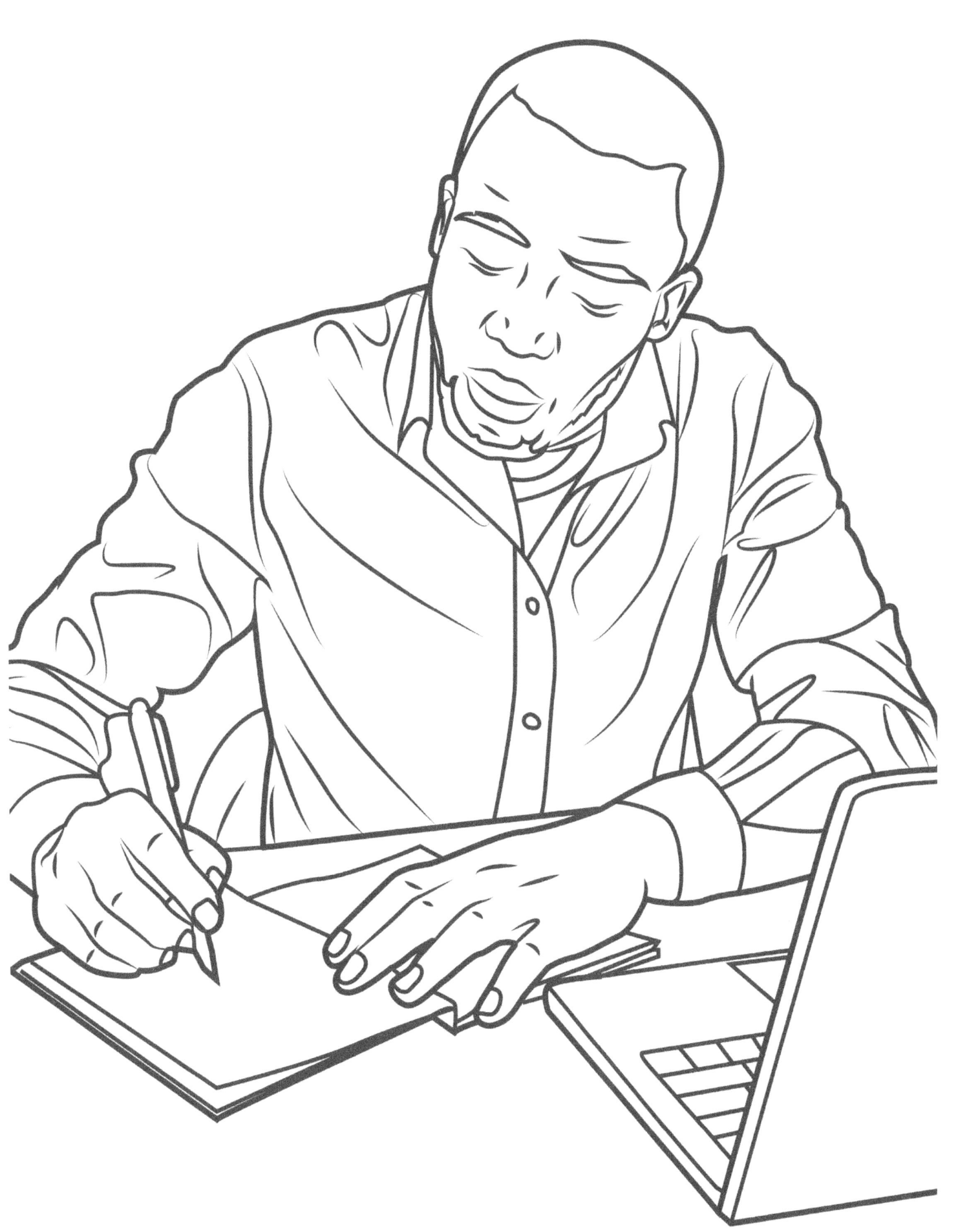

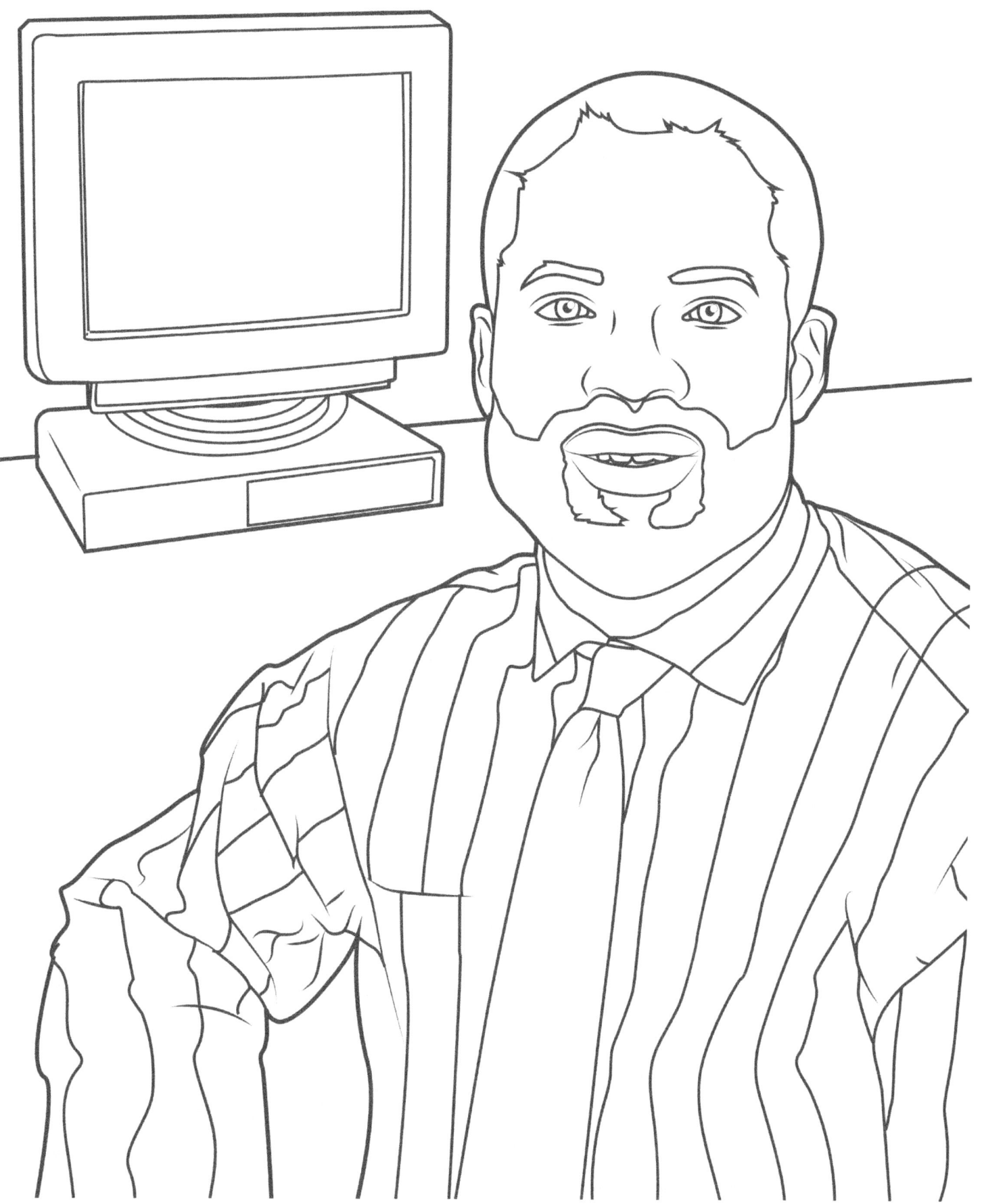

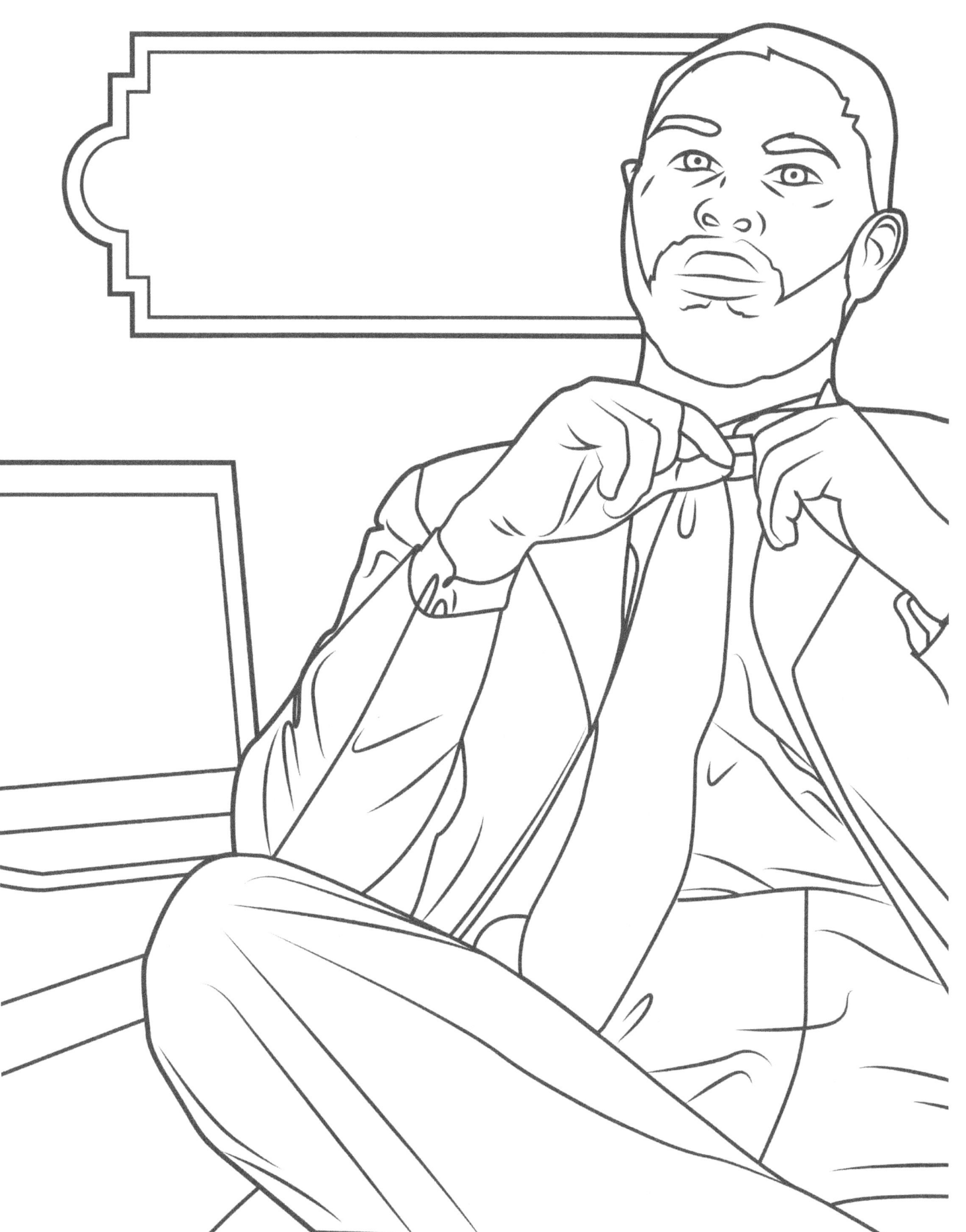

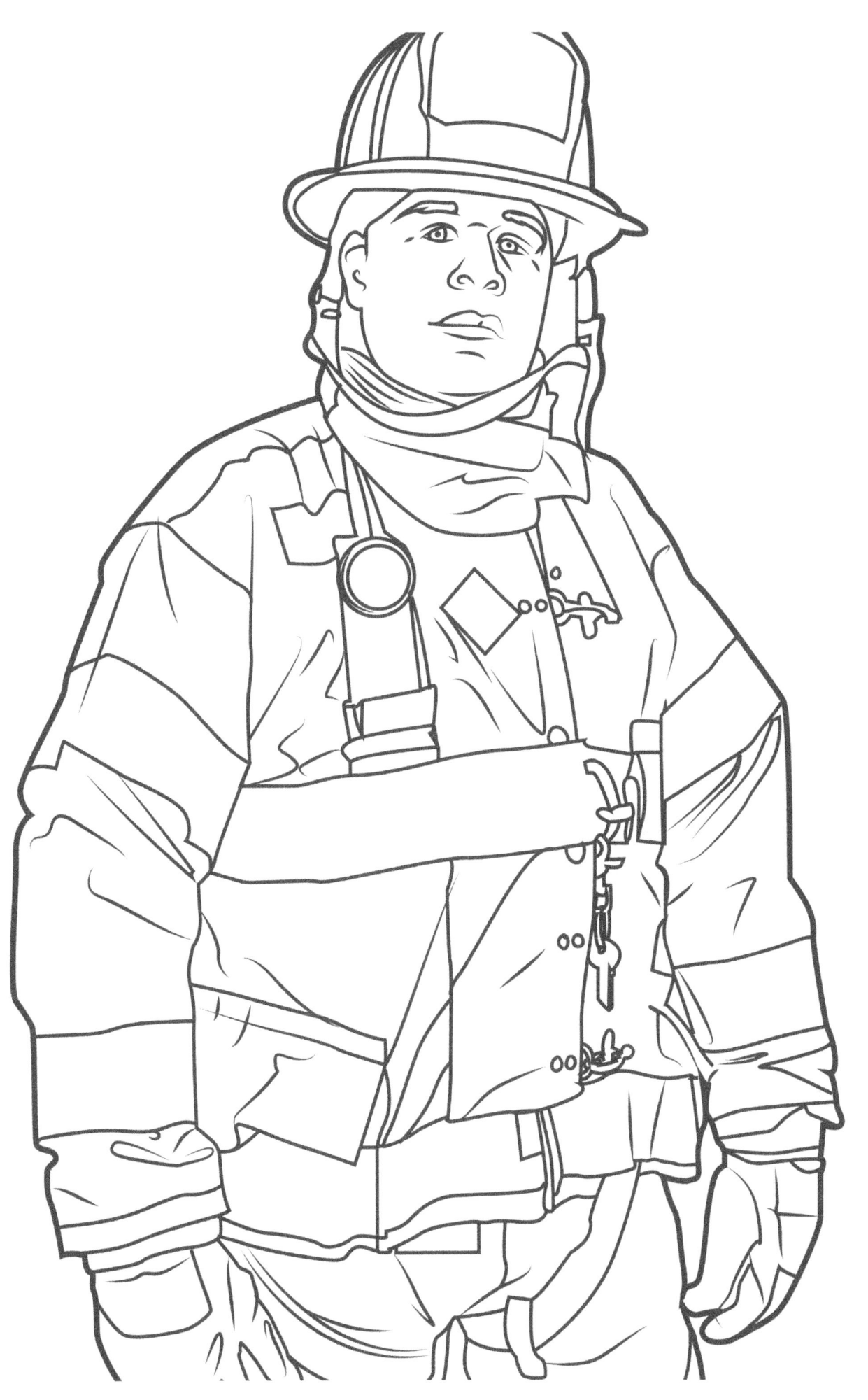

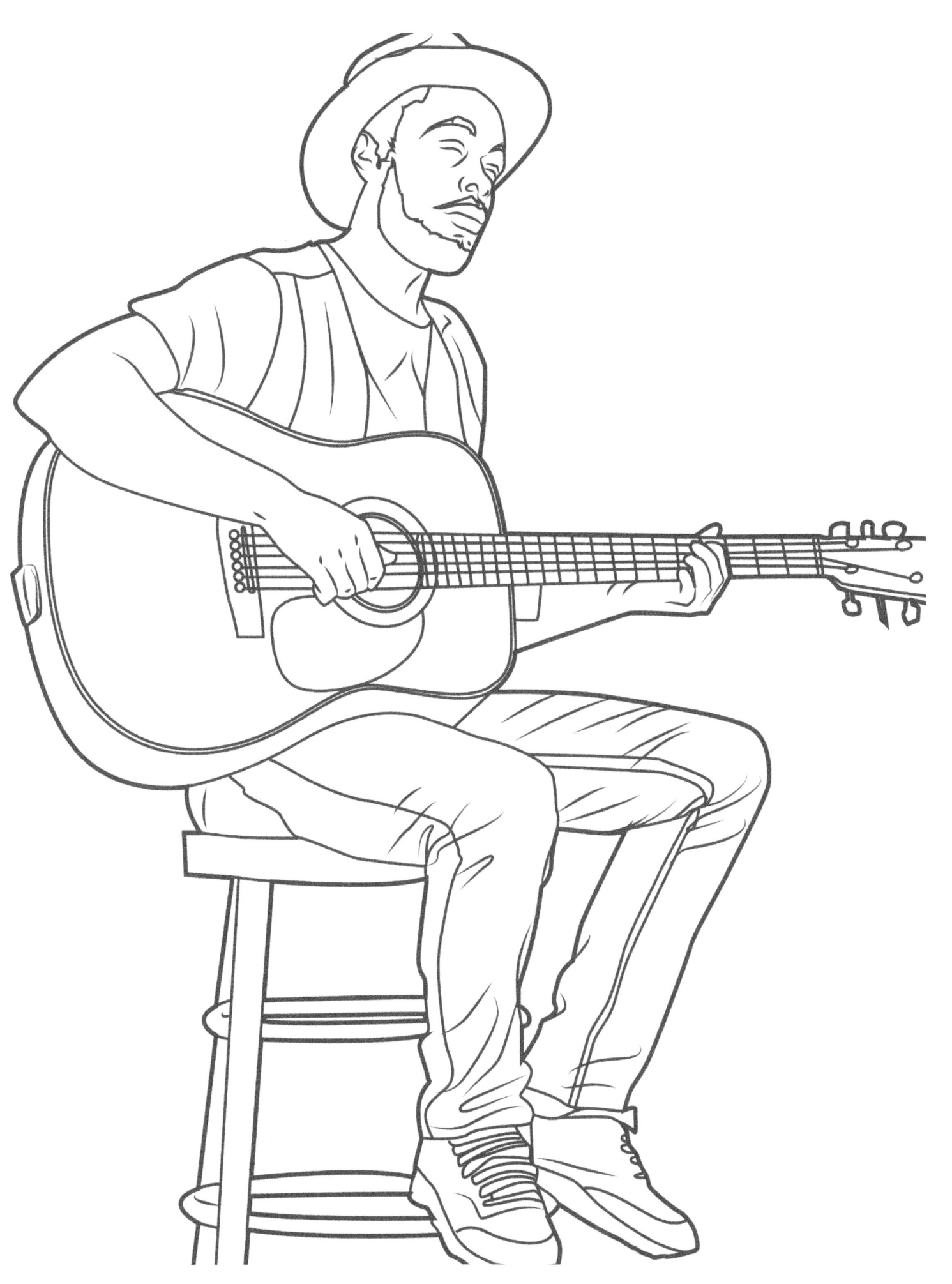

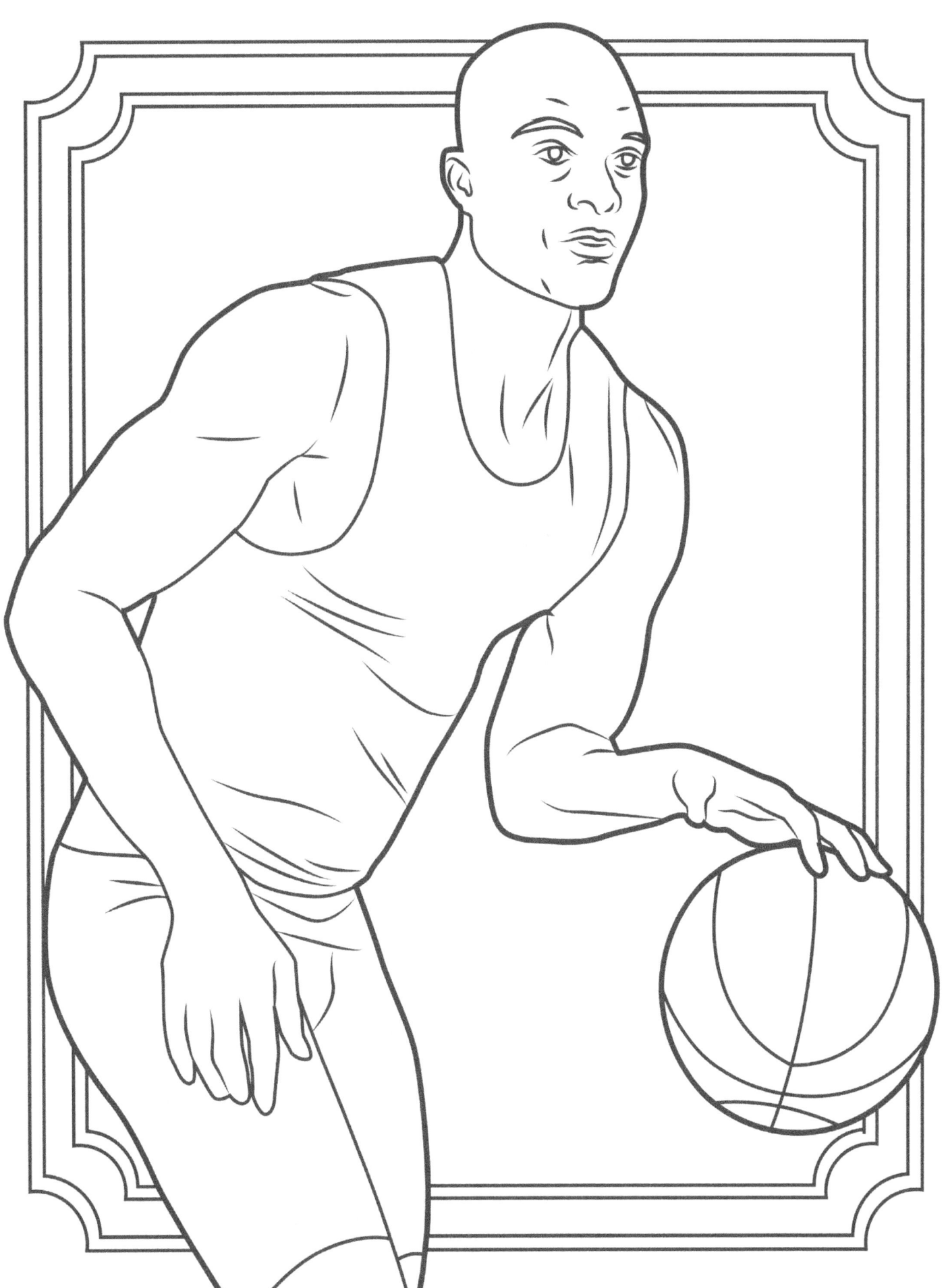

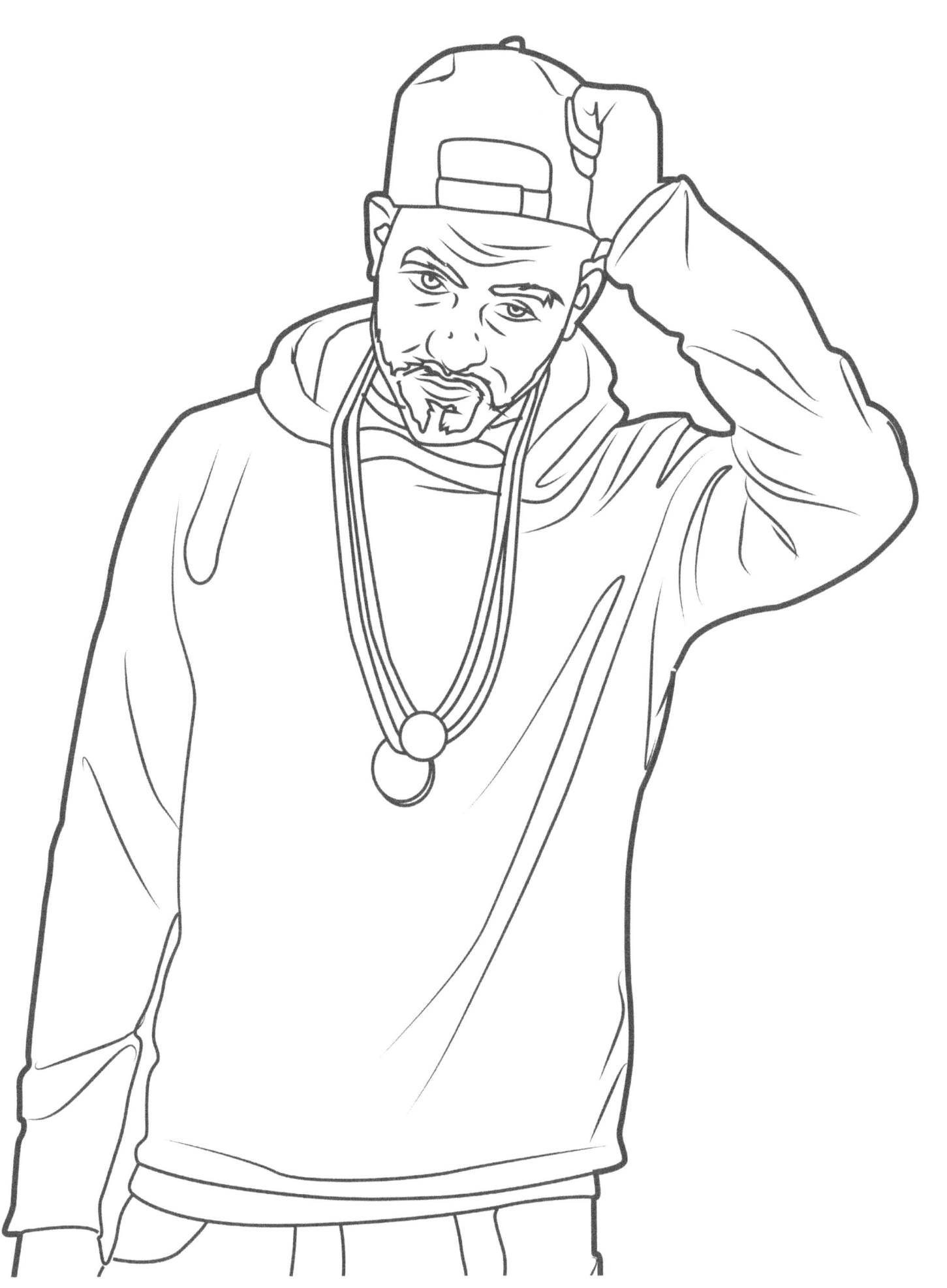

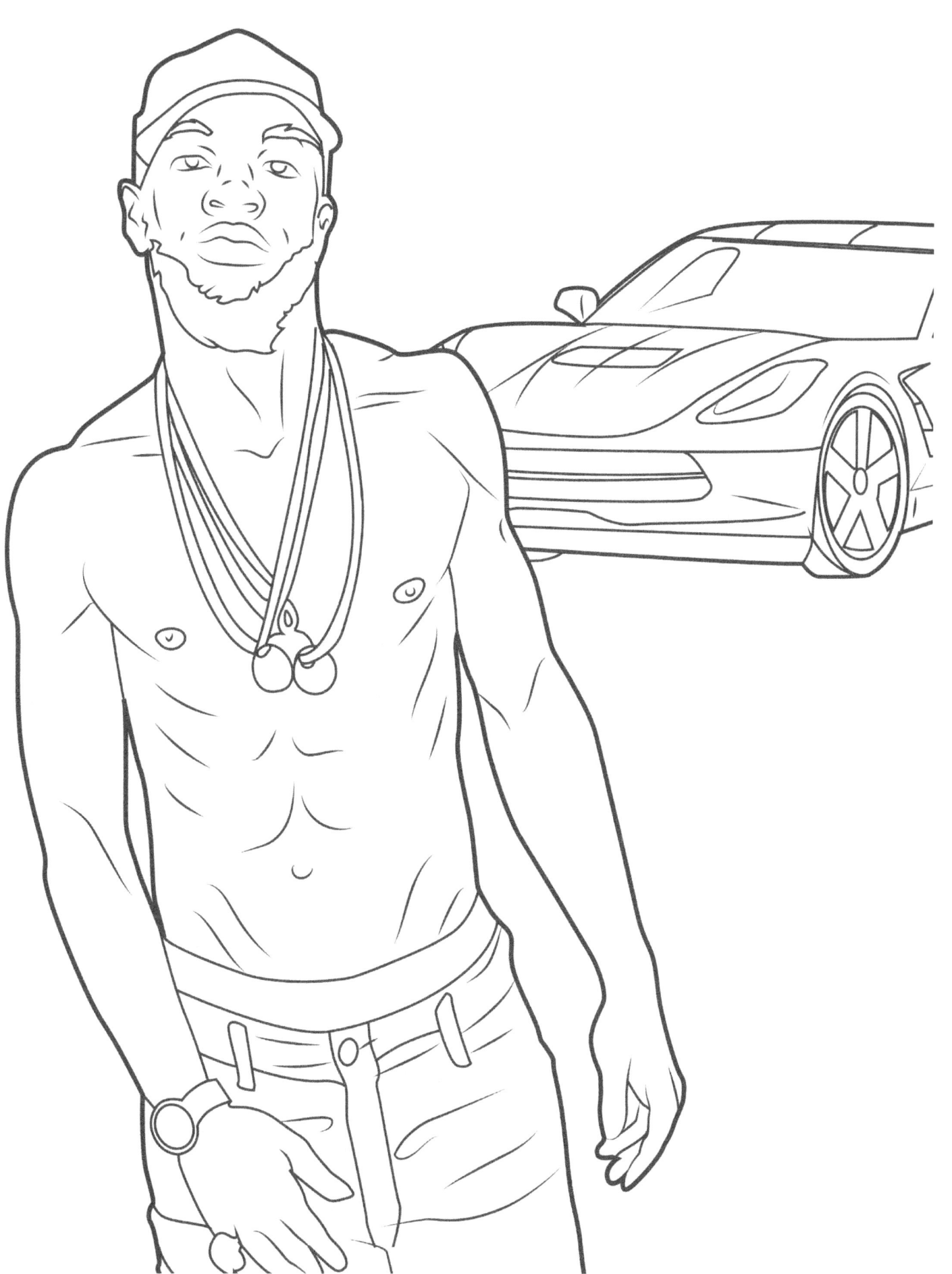

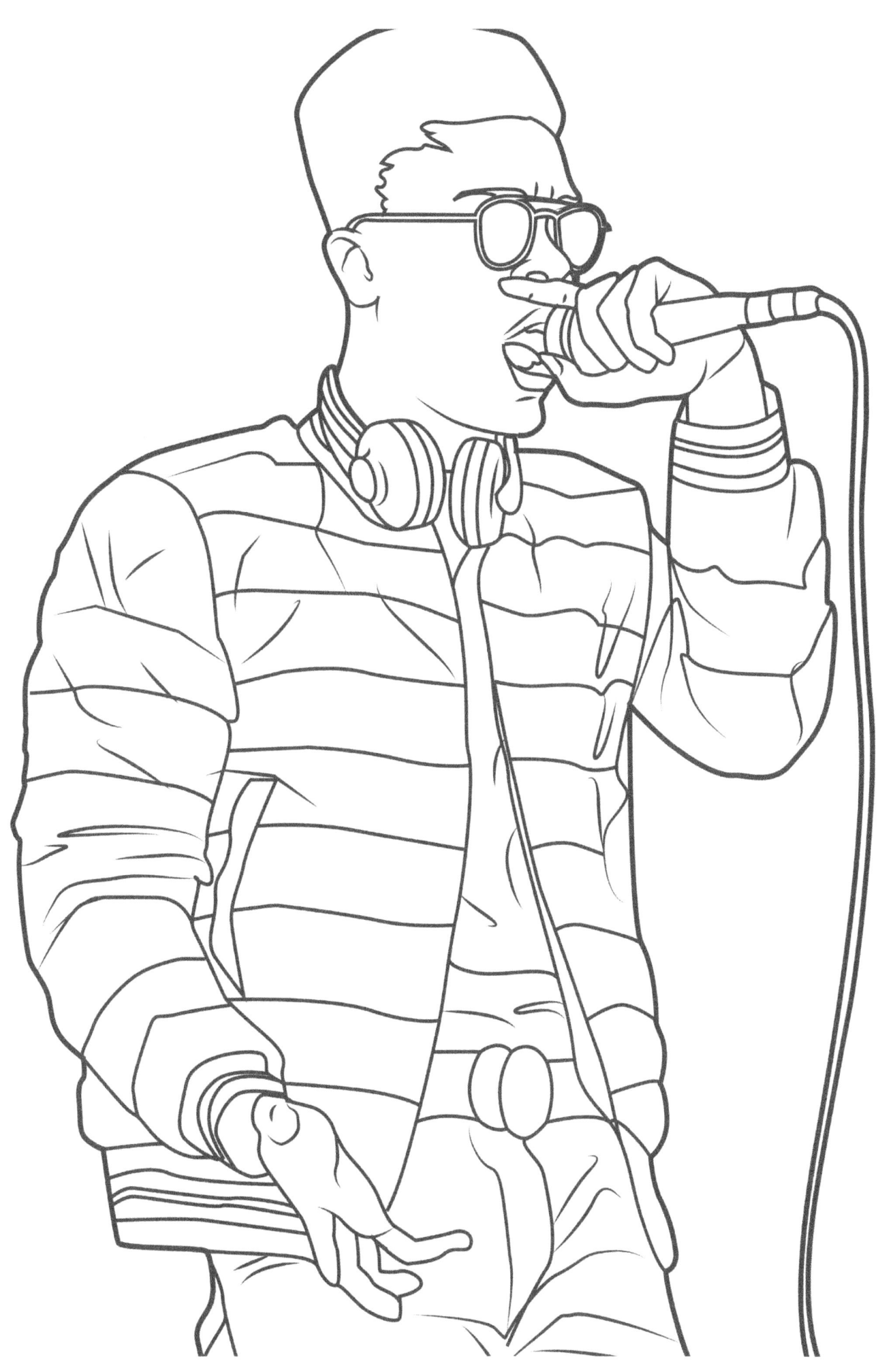

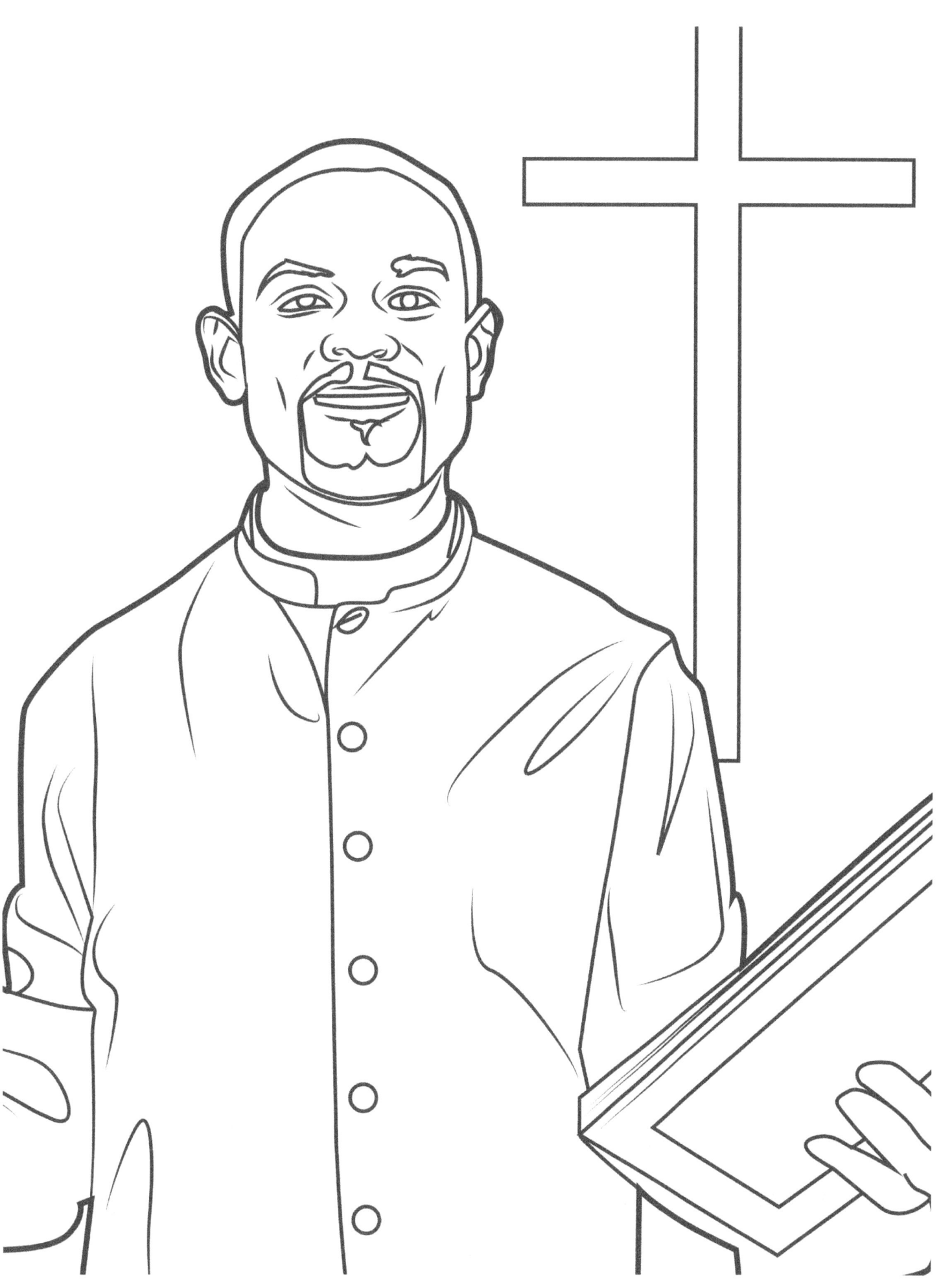

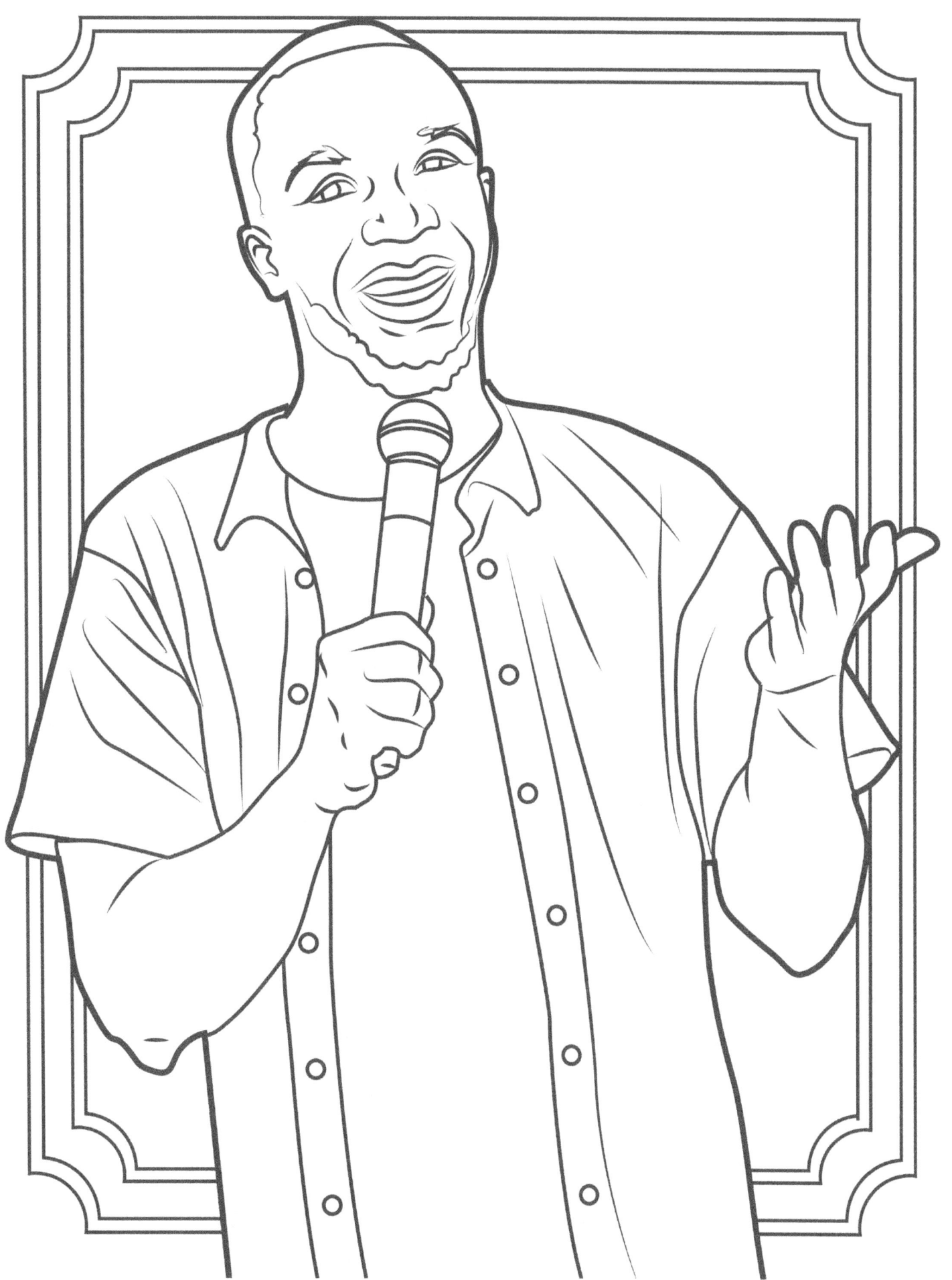

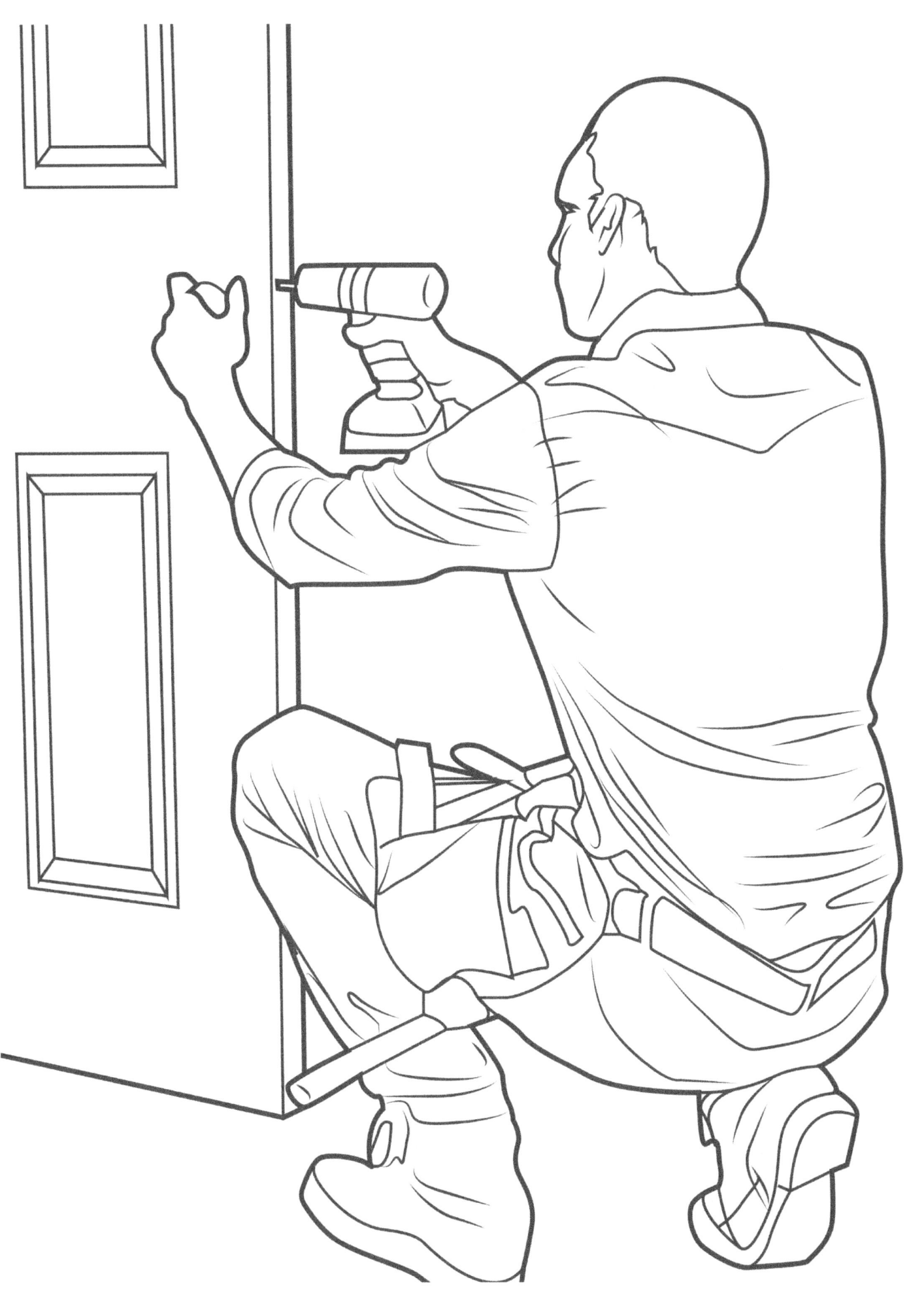

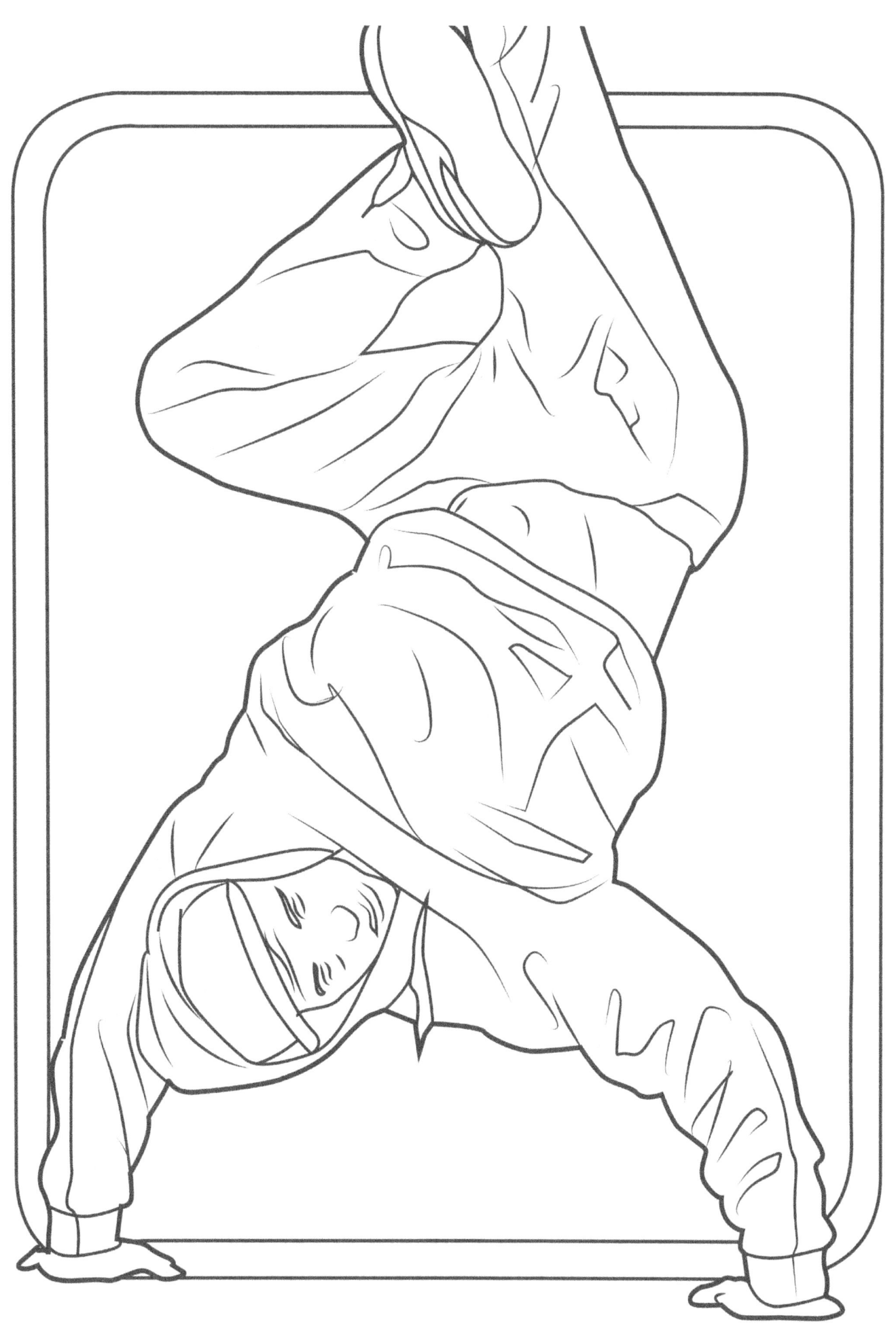

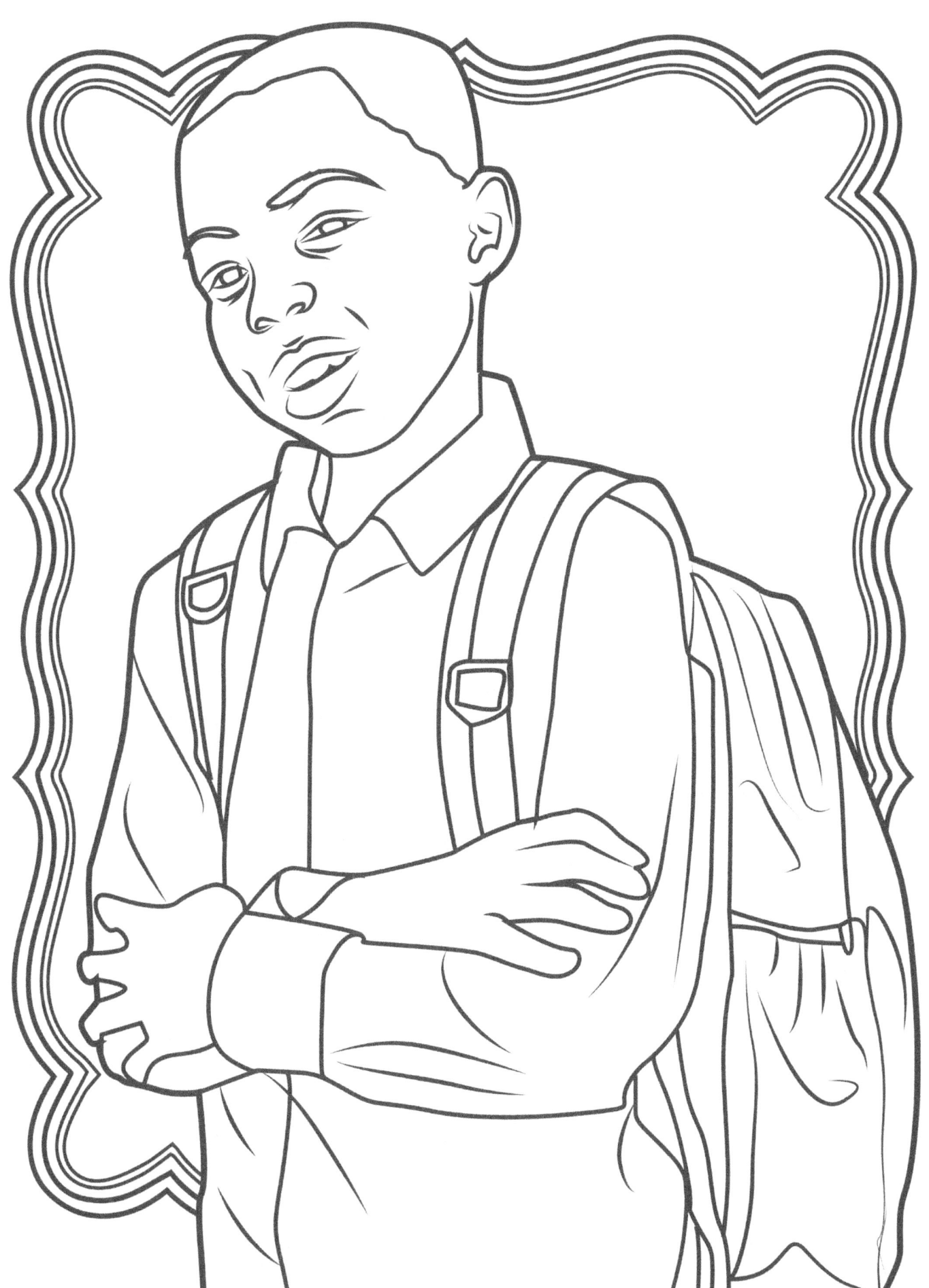

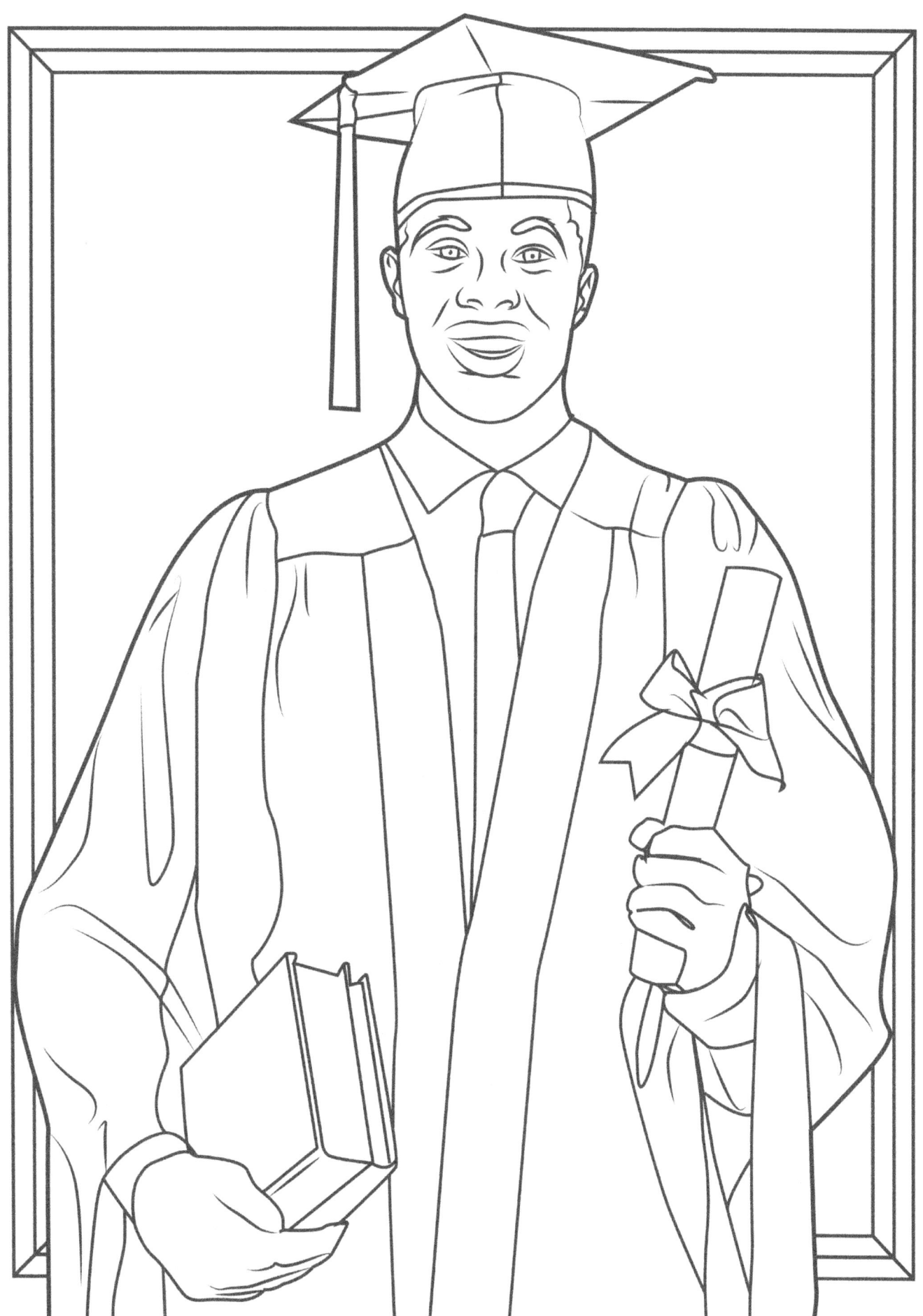

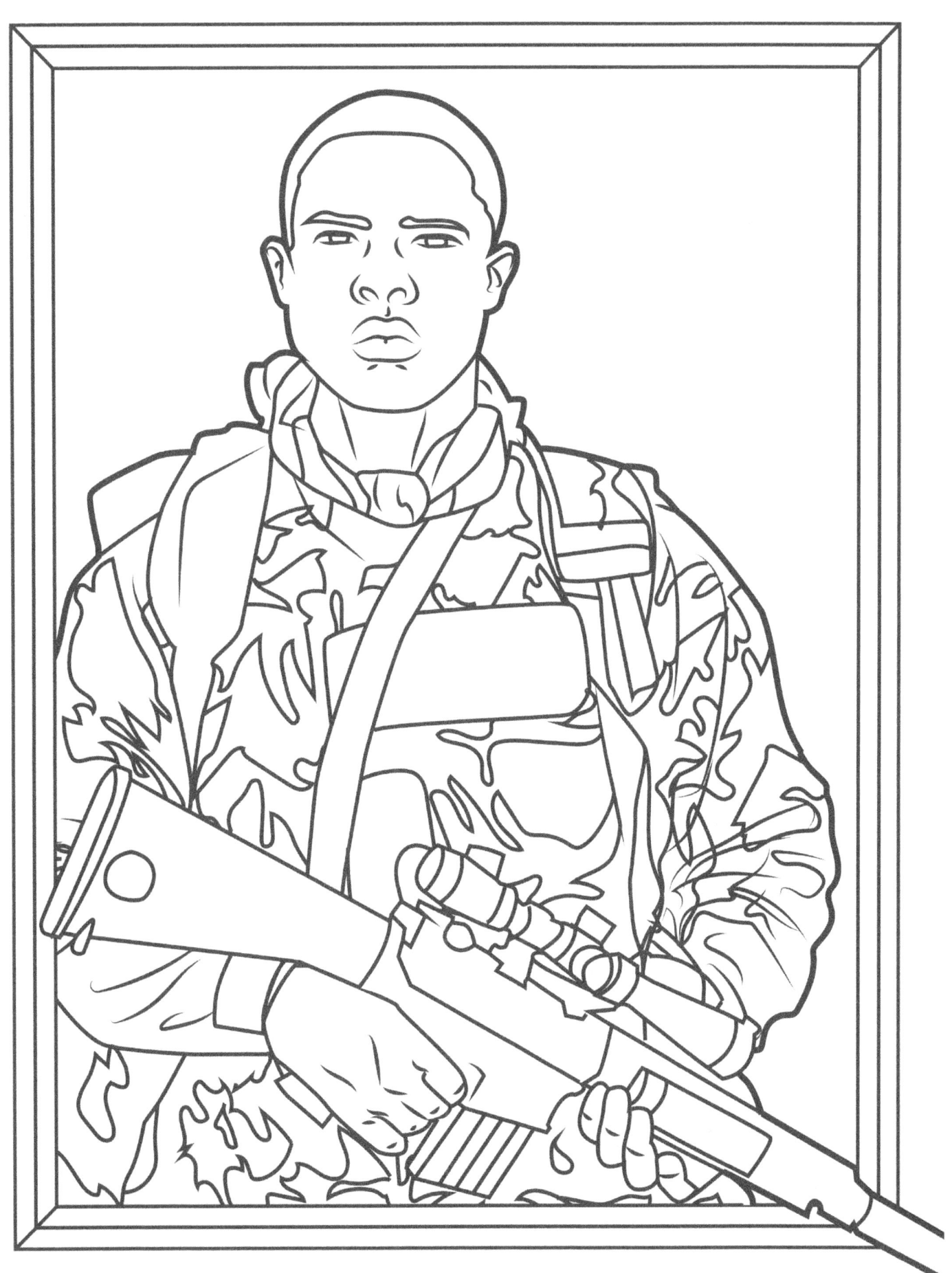

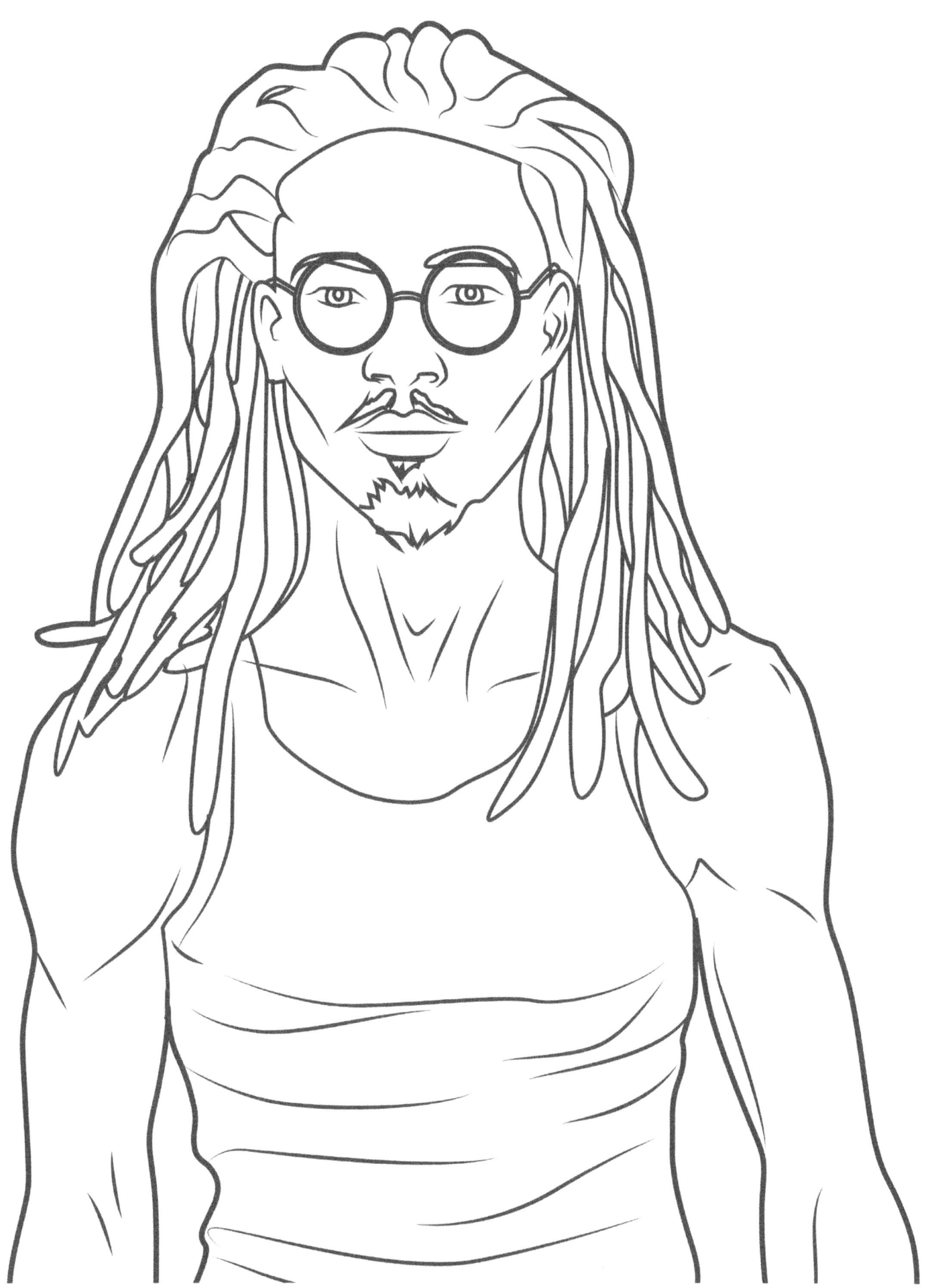

TOGETHER WE MAKE THE DIFFERENCE

If your actions
inspire others
to dream more,
learn more,
do more and
become more,
you are a leader

John Quincy Adams

DON'T JUDGE
EACH DAY BY
THE HARVEST
YOU REAP BUT
BY THE SEEDS
THAT YOU PLANT

ROBERT LOUIS
STEVENSON

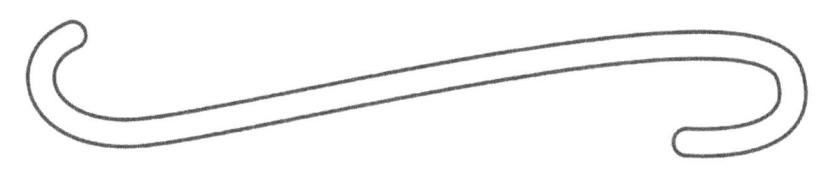

BELIEVE IN YOURSELF
AND ALL THAT YOU ARE.
KNOW THAT THERE IS
SOMETHING INSIDE OF
YOU THAT IS GREATER
THAN ANY OBSTACLE

CHRISTIAN D LARSON

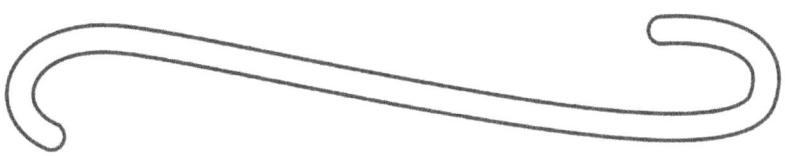

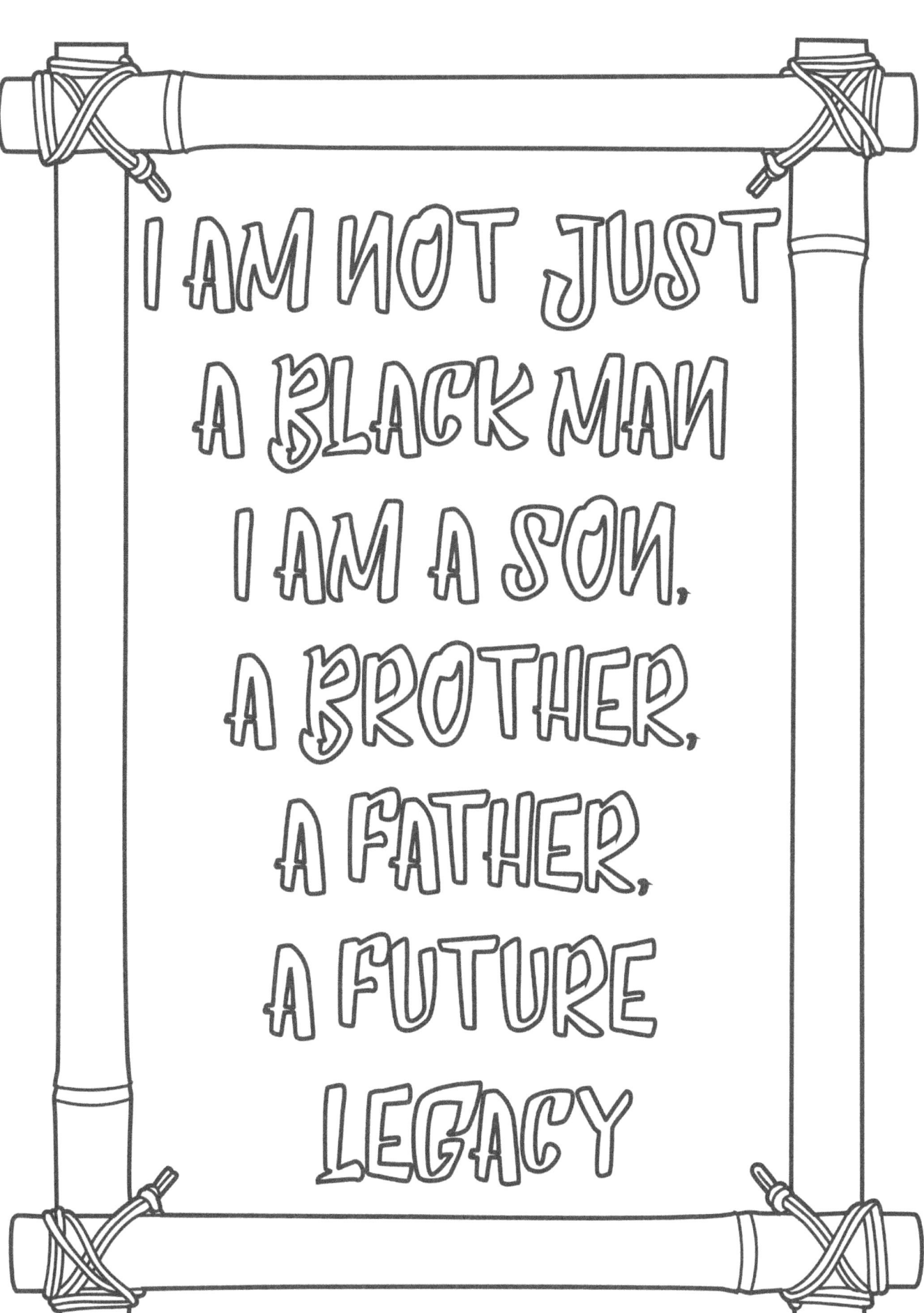

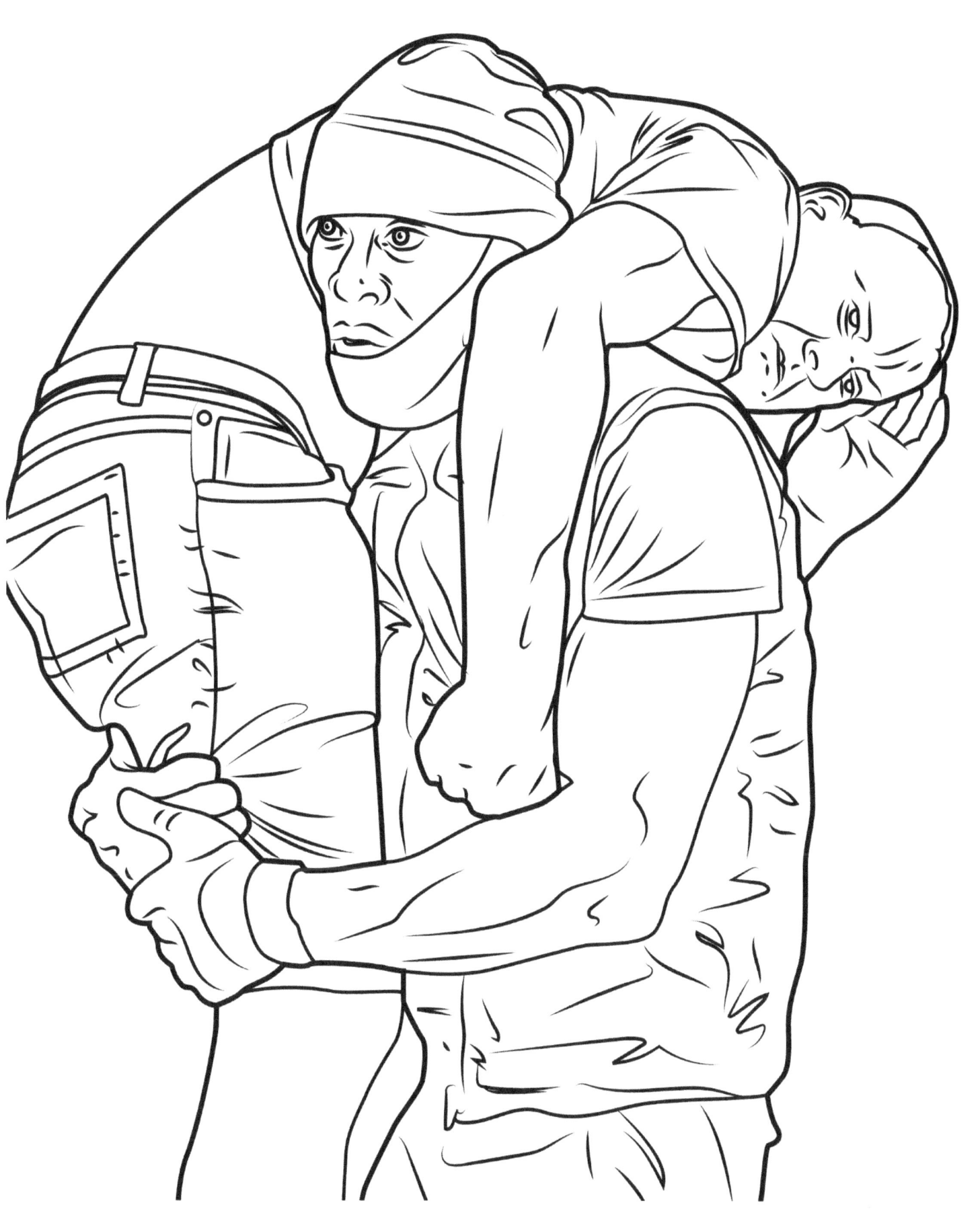

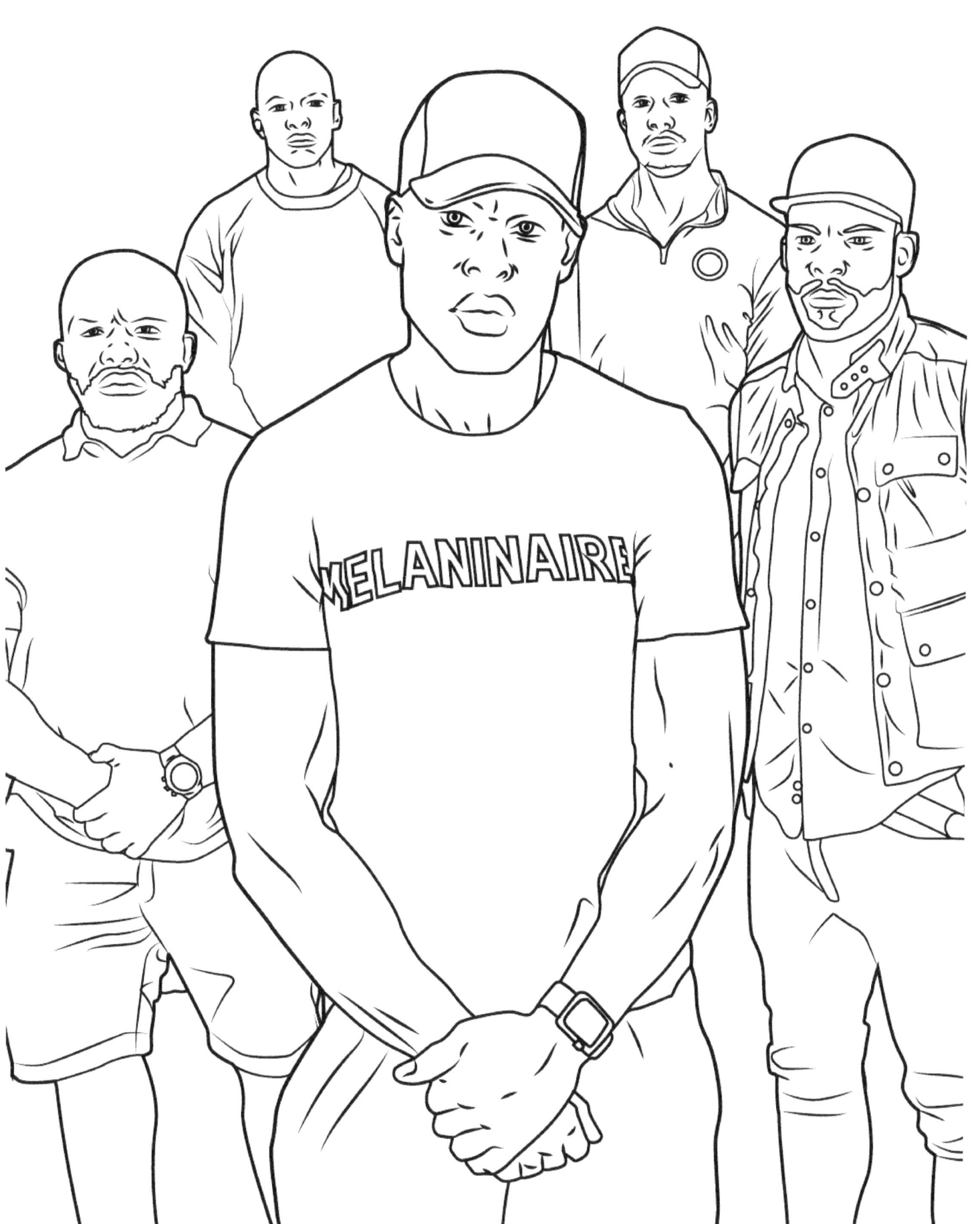

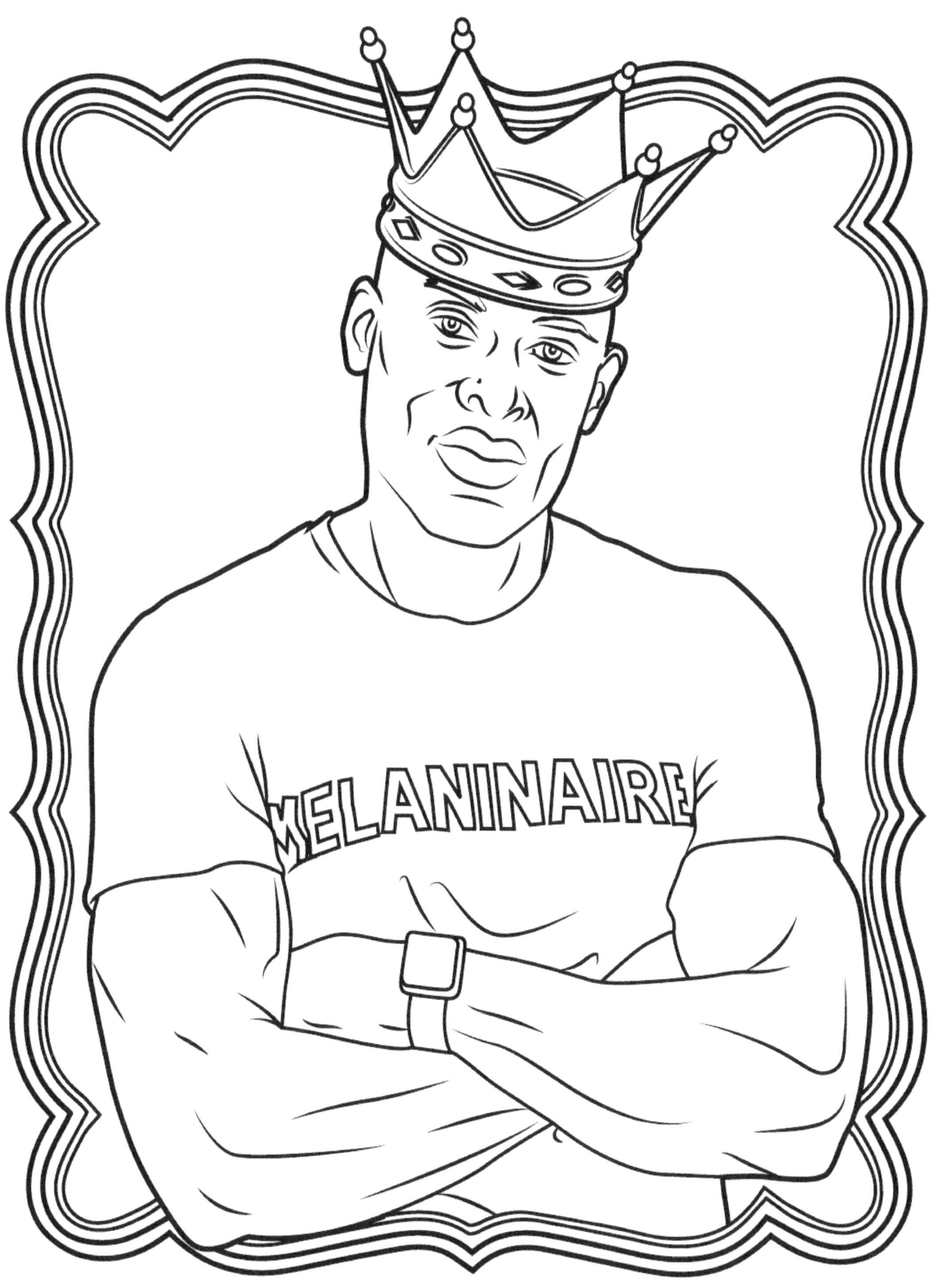

Other Coloring Books from Aryla Publishing

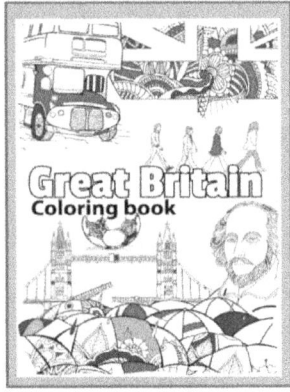
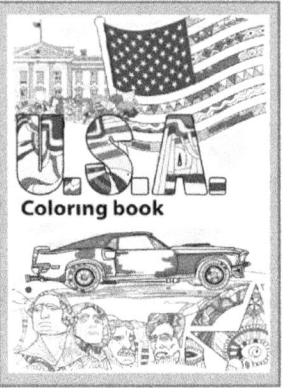
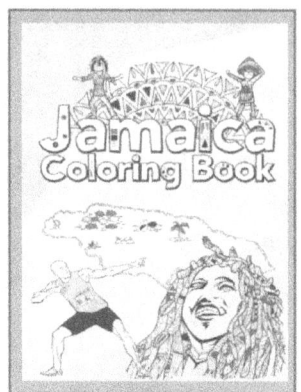
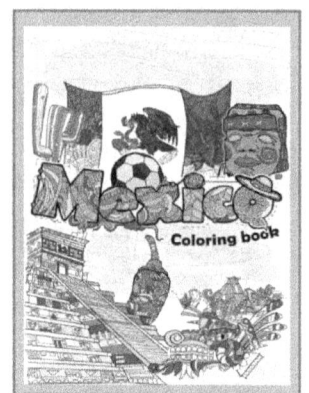

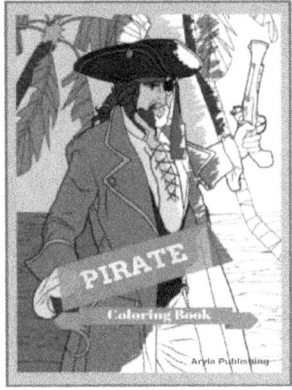
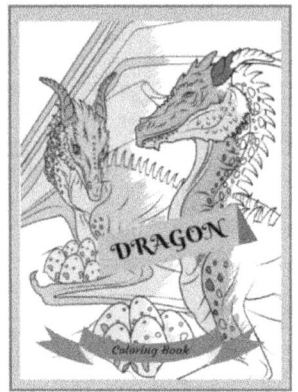
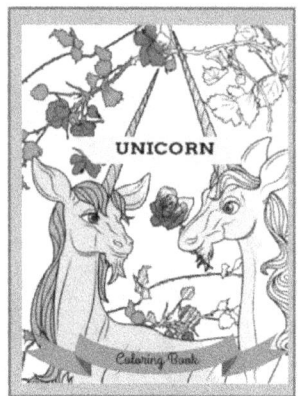
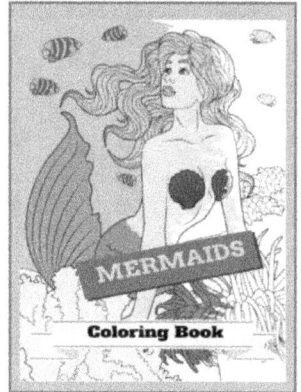

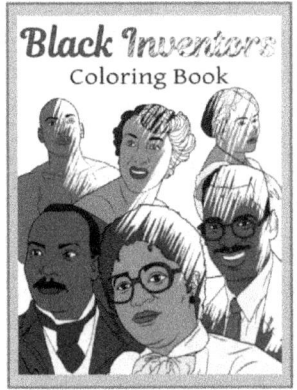
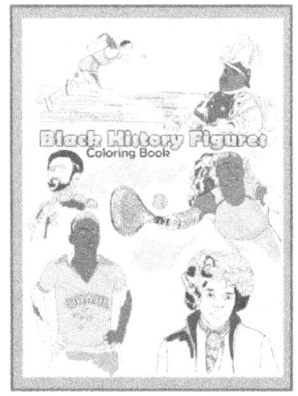
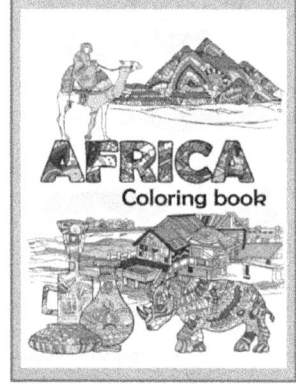
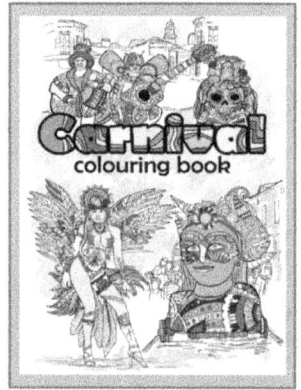

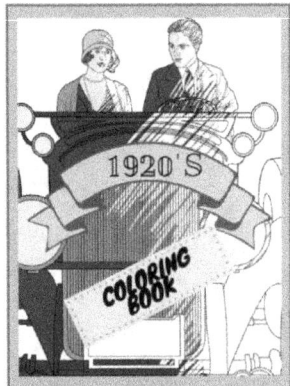
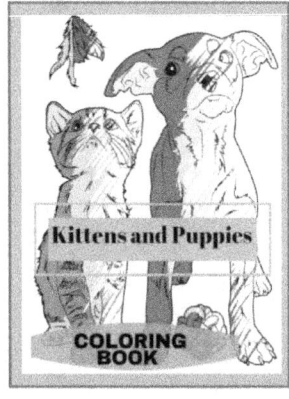
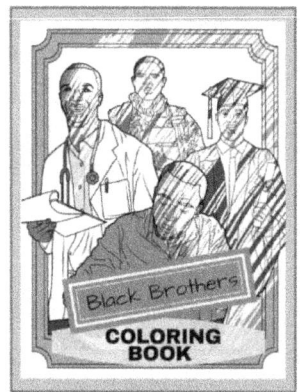
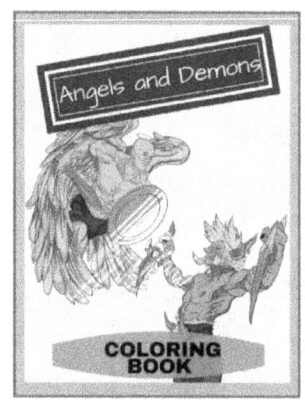

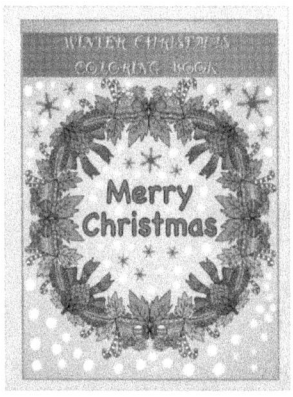
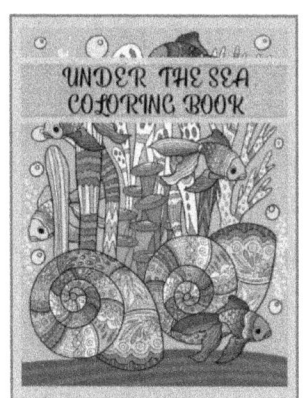
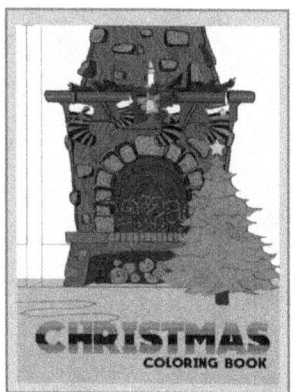
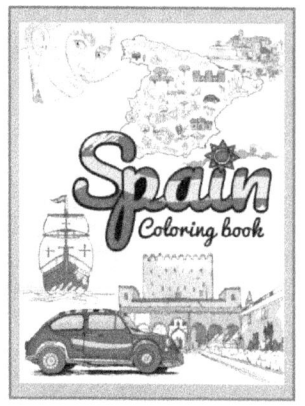
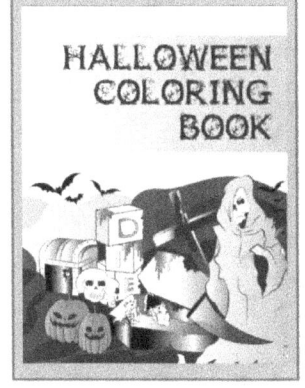
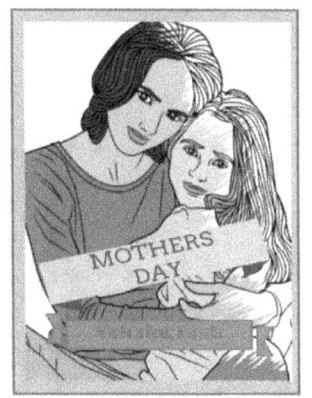
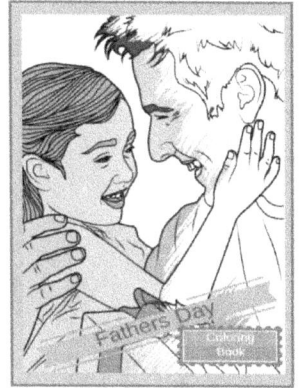
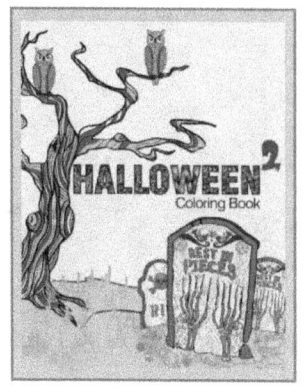
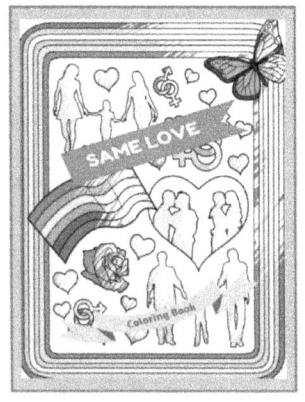
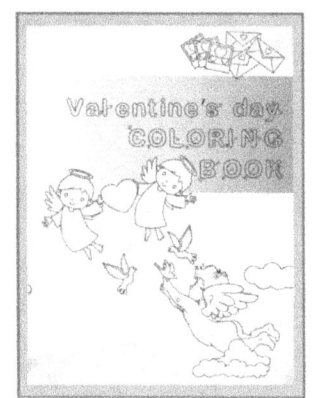
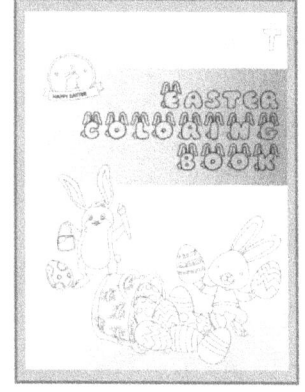
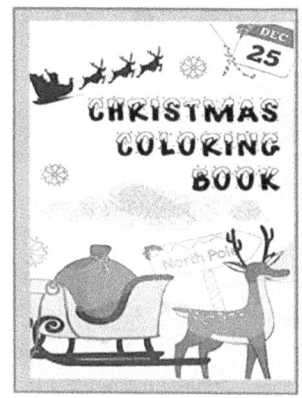
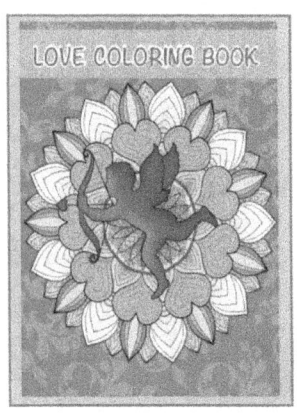
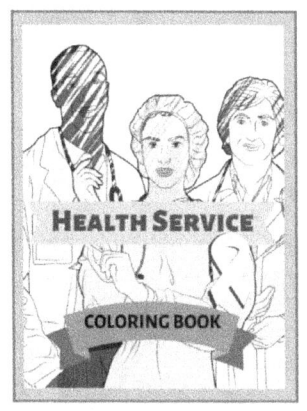
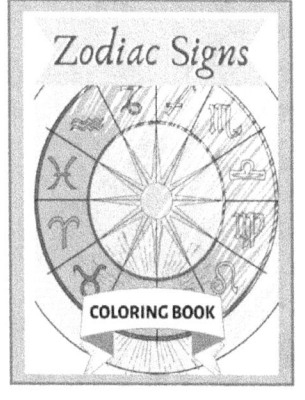
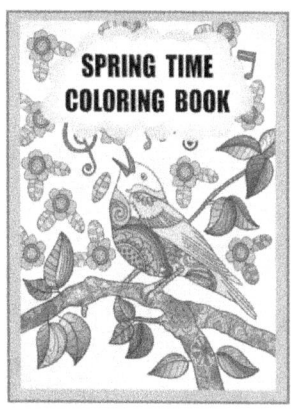

Color In Fun
Kids Books

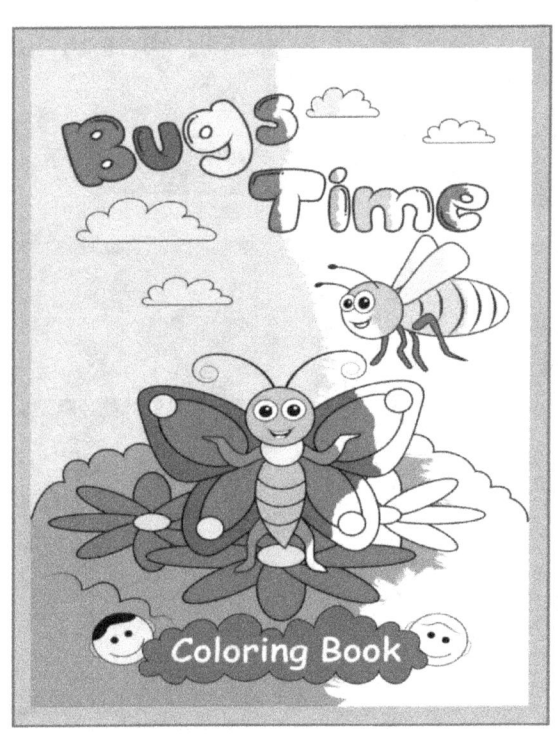

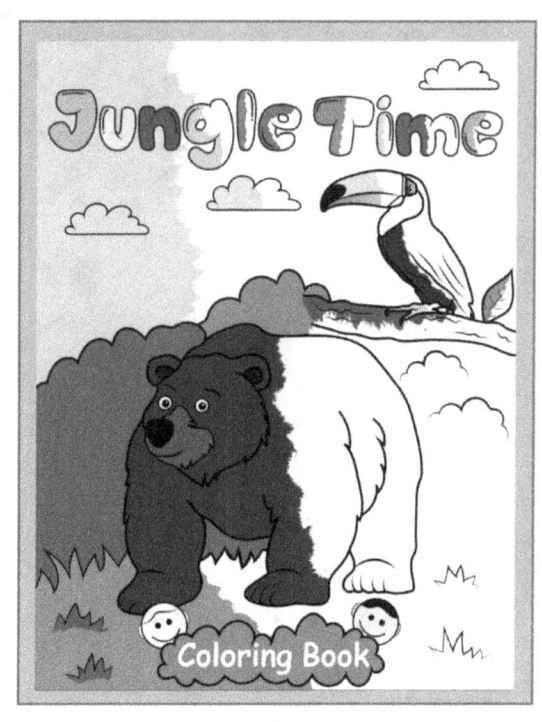

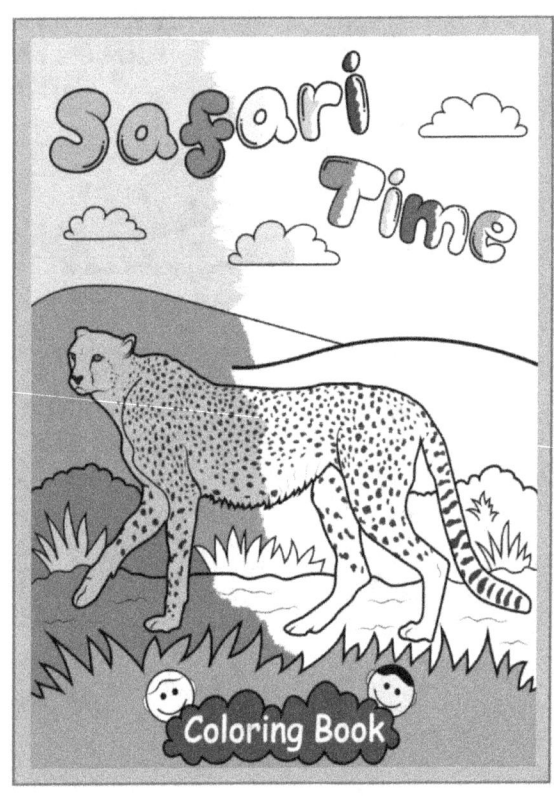

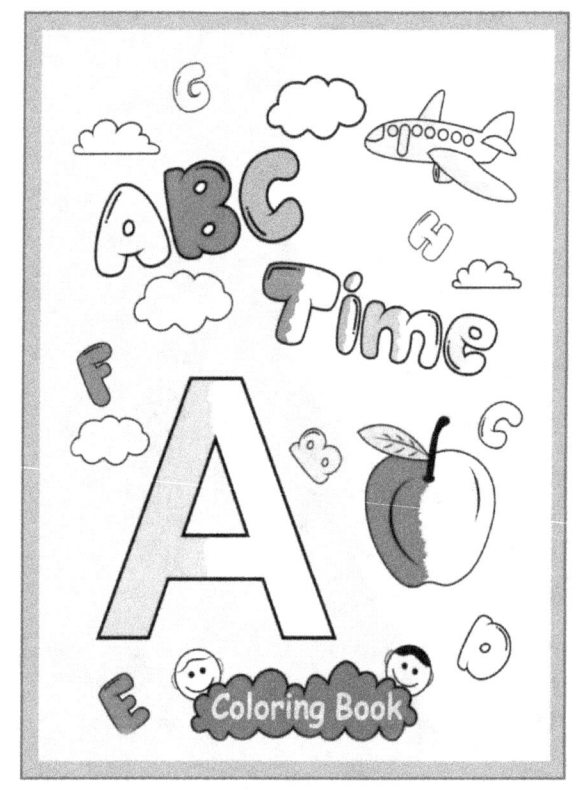

WE ARE ONE
Book Series

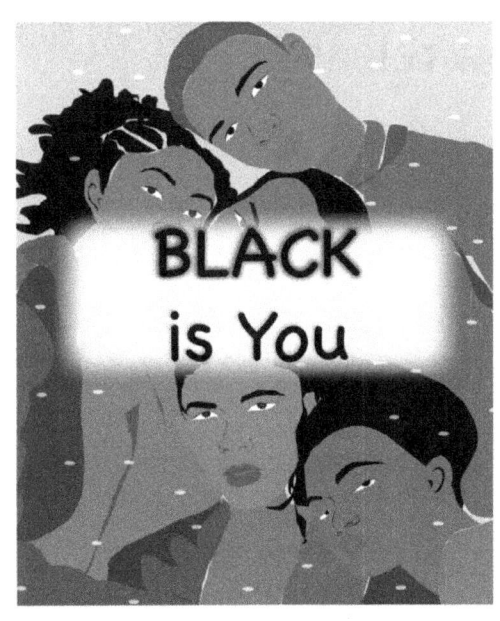

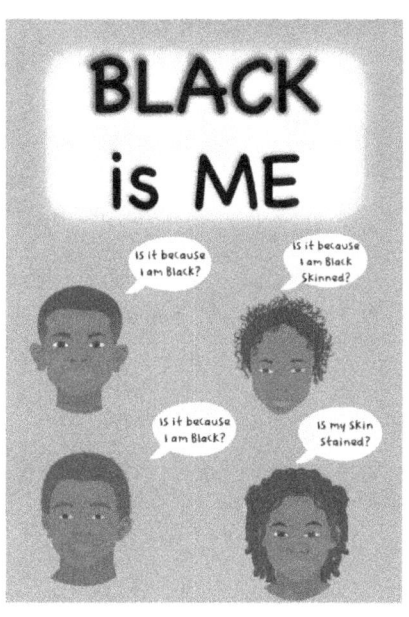

Visit **www.ArylaPublishing.com**

to find out about all new releases.

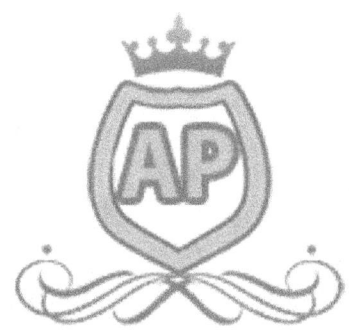

Follow us @arylapublishing on Twitter Instagram & Facebook

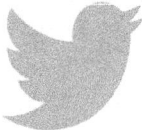  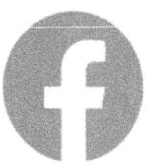

Search for Aryla Publishing on

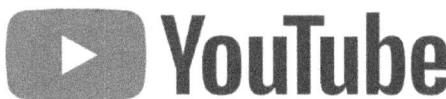 YouTube

Check out our _Book Trailers_

Subscribe **to keep up to date with new releases!**

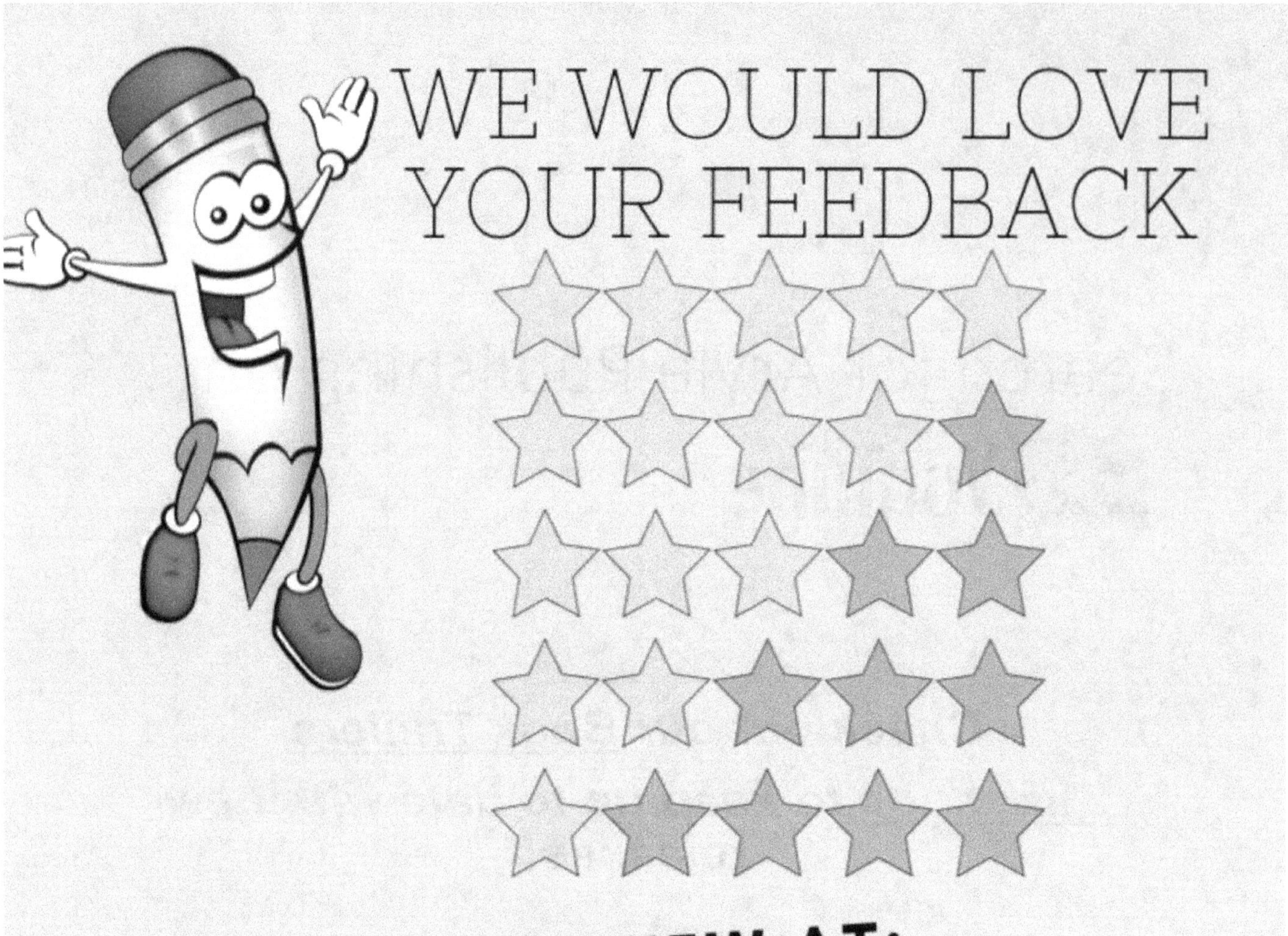

WE WOULD LOVE YOUR FEEDBACK

PLEASE LEAVE REVIEW AT:-

https://bit.ly/blackbrothersreview

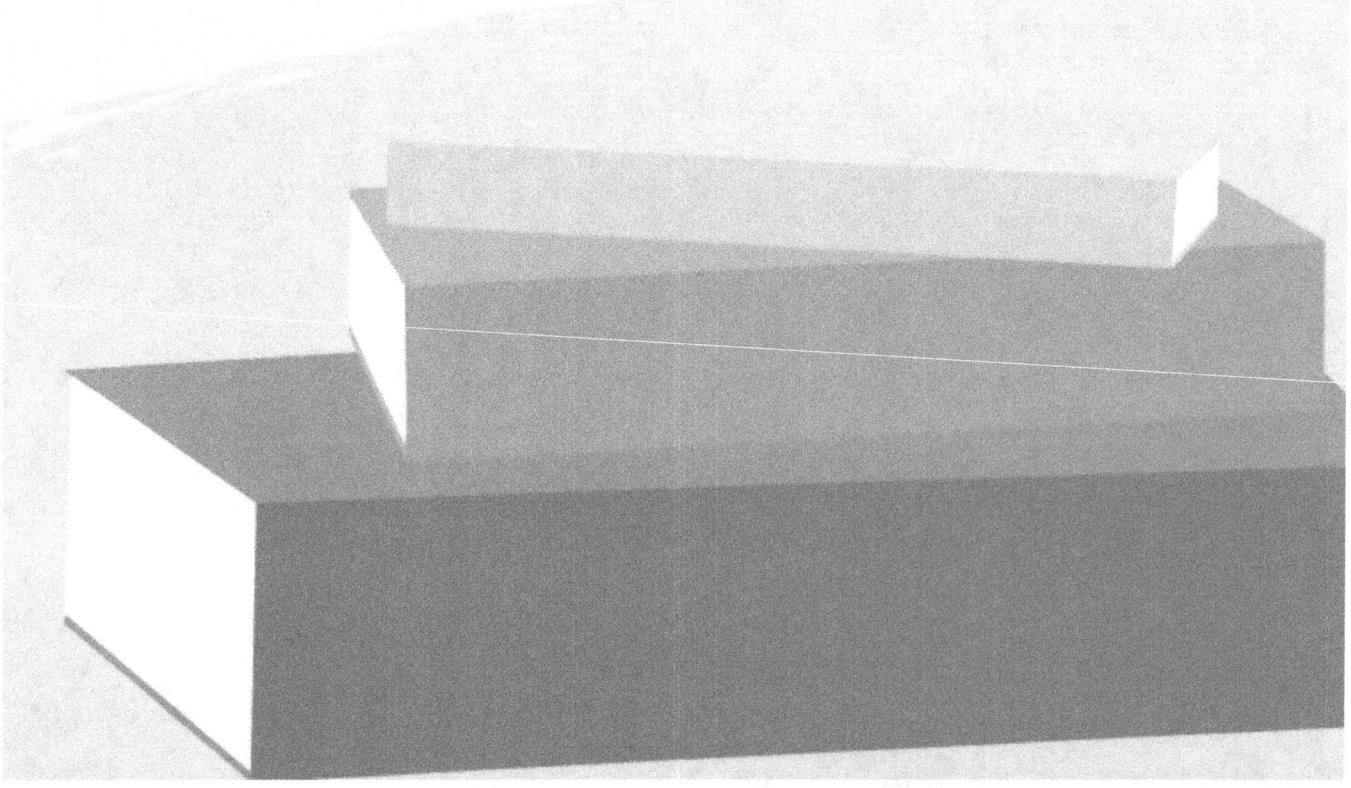